GARDENS OF BRITAIN

A Historic View

Patrick Taylor

GARDENS OF BRITAIN

A Historic View

INTERNATIONAL

GARDENS OF BRITAIN

Front Cover
Athelhampton House

Back Cover
Tresco Abbey

Editorial Director	Anne Zweibaum
Design, layout & cover	Christian Rondet
Editorial Assistant	Soline Massot
Copyeditor	Catherine Ferry and Marie-Paule Rochelois
Photoengraving	L'Exprimeur, Paris

Copyright © Vilo International, 25 rue Ginoux 75015 Paris, 2001
ISBN: 2-84576-036-1
Printed in Italy

Summary

Britain is remarkably rich in gardens, with admirable surviving examples from all periods since the sixteenth century. Various factors have contributed to this, of which the most important is very long periods of unbroken political and social stability. In addition to that, the principle of primogeniture, under which the eldest son inherits the family lands, has kept many great estates intact. Many of the historic gardens described in this book remain in the possession of the families that created them—such as Hatfield, Penshurst, Bramham and Bowood.

A profound influence on the fortunes of historic gardens in Britain has been that of the National Trust for England and Wales, and its counterpart in Scotland. Since 1947 the National Trust, founded to preserve the landscape and historic houses, has also occupied itself with gardens. It is a privately funded charity, with well over 2,000,000 members, which receives no state aid. Today it is the proprietor of the greatest collection of gardens ever gathered together under single owner-ship. It has pioneered the restoration of historic gardens and built up an unequalled expertise. Several of the gardens described in this book belong to the National Trust.

I have chosen my examples to illustrate the evolution in garden taste from the sixteenth century to the late twentieth century. Most of these gardens include, of course, features of different peri-ods. The gardens of Hampton Court, for example, go back to the early sixteenth century and contain features of virtually all the chief period styles up to the twentieth century. All the gardens are regularly open to the public and opening details are given in an appendix on page 157.

Britain is essentially a conservative country and, certainly in the case of garden design, has rarely been strongly influenced by the avant garde. Plantsmanship has a profoundly important position in British horticulture. Gardens such as Hatfield, Caerhays Castle, Tresco Abbey and Beth Chatto's garden are all remarkable collections of plants as well as being beautiful landscapes. Although Britain has a small native flora, with only around 1,300 native flow-ering plants of which only a handful are endemic, the climate will sustain a wider diversity of plants than any other in the world. It is estimated that around 150,000 garden plants (including, of course, cultivars) are grown in British gardens. This desire to collect and study plants has had a crucial influence on garden design. The naturalistic garden (of which Caerhays is a good example) is one response to the problem of accommodating plants har-moniously, and the Arts and Crafts style of such gardens as Great Dixter and Crathes Castle, is another. The latter, with its sequences of garden 'rooms', has its origins in the Italian Renaissance, like many another essential ideas in garden design. A new influence is what one might call the ecological garden, of which Beth Chatto's garden is an exceptional example. Here, there is an underlying concern for the environment, regarding the garden as a partnership with nature rather than a battle against it.

The single most influential British garden style—and I should call it English, for it is not really found in Scotland and Wales—is the 18th-century landscape park. Several are

left

The Topiary garden at Great Dixter

described here—Studley Royal, Stowe, Stourhead, Bowood and Hestercombe. Capability Brown designed over 130 landscapes, many of which survive more or less intact. He had a profound influence on the appearance of the English countryside and his ideas spread all over Europe. Although untrained—in the eighteenth century there was no training available for garden designers—he was, in the execution of his work, a full-blown professional landscape architect. Many of the greatest garden makers were pure amateurs and the only garden they ever created was for themselves. Lord Benson at Bramham Park, the Aislabies, father and son, at Studley Royal, the Hoare family at Stourhead and the Burnetts at Crathes, were all amateurs. The deeply learned gentleman plantsman or landscaper is a treasured figure in British garden history. The great patrons of the major plant-hunting expeditions—the Williamses at Caerhays or the Smiths at Tresco—were all amateurs.

A garden feature that seems to have first been codified in Britain is that of the herbaceous and latterly, the mixed, border. The deep border, with swathes of herbaceous perennials, often chosen with a skilful eye for colour harmonies, does not appear in British gardens before the latter part of the nineteenth century. Its greatest practitioner and theoretician was Gertrude Jekyll, another garden amateur, although she trained as an artist. The border is probably the commonest single feature of British gardens, frequently appearing quite unhistorically (at Montacute, for example), making an ornamental new addition to an old layout. In Beth Chatto's garden the idea of the border is reinvigorated in an unexpected fashion.

In the late twentieth century, although there are one or two distinctive avant garde gardens, such as Charles Jencks's extraordinary landscape in the Keswick estate in the Scottish borders and Ian Hamilton Finlay's mesmerisingly poetic garden at Little Sparta, they seem to have sprung fully formed from the inventiveness of their creators. At the moment, apart from their beauty, their most striking characteristic is their uniqueness. It is too early to say if such experiments will inspire a following—there is no sign of it yet. It is, perhaps, arguably a deficiency of British garden culture that we should look so fondly towards the past. But when the past is so rich in surviving beauties it is easier to forgive this backward-looking tendency.

facing page on the left
The sunken garden at Hampton
Court (top)
One of the terrace borders at
Powis Castle (middle)
View of the patte d'oie at
Hampton Court (bottom)

facing page on the right
An early eighteenth century stone
ornament at Bramham Park (top)
A putto at Crathes Castle (bottom)

Hatfield House

Hatfield House

double staircase from the terrace
in the East Gardens

<u>right</u>
The north façade of Hatfield House
from the Knot Garden

<u>left</u>
The East Gardens with rows
of clipped holm oaks

One of the most attractive types of garden in Britain is the historic estate which displays gardening styles of different periods held together by firm design. Hatfield House in Hertfordshire, just north of London, is an exceptional example. The house was built for Robert Cecil between 1607 and 1612. His father, Lord Burghley, had been Queen Elizabeth I's most important secretary of state, a powerful position which Robert Cecil took over on his father's death and carried on under a very different monarch, James I, on Queen Elizabeth's death in 1603.

Gardening was in Robert Cecil's blood. As a young man he had designed a garden to celebrate the Queen's visit to his father's house in 1591. This, in characteristically Renaissance style, was full of symbolism: 'the Virtues were done in roses ... the Graces of pansies party-coloured . . . an arbour all of eglantine.' Roses were particularly associated with the virgin Queen, as they are with the Virgin Mary. When Cecil started work at Hatfield he brought with him gardeners from his previous estate at Theobalds. They started work on the new garden in 1609, long before the new house was completed. The following year they were joined by a figure of central importance in English horticulture, John Tradescant the Elder, who in due course became gardener to King James I's successor, Charles I.

Tradescant was a deeply learned plantsman who introduced many new plants to English gardens through his connections all over Europe. Furthermore, as a member of the Virginia Company, he was able to acquire North American plants which had never been seen in any European garden. The archives still preserved at Hatfield show the scale and ambitions of Tradescant's activities. He notes the acquisition of 'many rare shrubs given me by Master Robyns.' This was Jean Robin, royal gardener to King Henri III of France—*arboriste et simpliciste du roi* - and first director of the Jardin des Plantes in Paris on its foundation in 1626.

Tradescant was very much the plantsman and practical horticulturist rather than a garden designer. One of the most fascinating figures to be associated with the layout of the gardens at Hatfield

A central path links the Old Palace
garden's compartments

right
The Old Palace garden with its
central fountain

below

An intricate pattern of box-edged
compartments in the Old Palace
garden

was Salomon de Caus, a Frenchman who was associated with several notable European gardens in the early seventeenth century. At Hatfield he devised an ornamental water garden overlooked by a banqueting house for which a drawing, dated 1611, still survives in the Hatfield archives.

The pattern of formal gardens about the house at Hatfield survived well into the eighteenth century but, by the end of the century, this had been swept away and replaced with a landscape park, running up to the walls of the house. In the 1840s, however, the Marquess of Salisbury reinstated the seventeenth century formal layout, following the original foundations of the walls. It is this essential pattern that may be seen in the garden today. In 1972 the present Marchioness of Salisbury came to live at Hatfield and has had a profound influence on the present character of the garden. She is a deeply knowledgeable practical gardener who has immersed herself in the history of the gardens at Hatfield and in garden history generally. Before her husband inherited Hatfield she had been the châtelaine of another Cecil house, the exquisite Cranborne Manor in Dorset, where she revitalised a remarkable garden. Cranborne, however, is a relatively small garden while at Hatfield the formal gardens which encircle the house cover an area of 30 acres.

The garden which may be seen today follows a pattern which was determined in the early seventeenth century. But, although Lady Salisbury wanted to honour the history of the garden, she had no desire to attempt to recreate a purist historical layout. The existing partitions of walls, hedges and paths provided an admirable framework for the lively planting which she introduced. She has also created entirely new gardens, making reference to the past and taking advantage of the fine historic setting. In the grounds of the house, for example, is the much earlier Hatfield Old Palace, a handsome brick building going back to the late fifteenth century. In front of it, on the site of a nineteenth century rose garden, she laid out a sunken garden from whose raised walks visitors may look down on a lovely, intricate pattern of beds—a characteristically Tudor device. Here Lady Salisbury has laid out four box-edged enclosures with a fountain at the centre. Here is a maze, and parterres in the form of a knot gardens using plants from the sixteenth, seventeenth, and eighteenth centuries. Several of these plants are particularly associated with Tradescant, such as *Tradescantia virginiana* and *Aster tradescantii,* which he introduced from America.

13

Hatfield House

To one side of the Old Palace are the Privy Garden and the Scented Garden both of which date back to the early seventeenth century. Some of the old planting has been preserved, such as an eighteenth century lime walk in the Privy Garden, but most of it has been redone by Lady Salisbury. The borders of the privy garden are a distinctive late twentieth century mixture of herbaceous and woody plants, planned to flower over a very long period. Among the plants used here are the new David Austin 'English Roses', which have the scent and character of old roses but are perpetual flowering.

facing page
Exuberant planting
at the centre of the Privy Garden

below
Lilium regale adds rich perfume
to the Scented Garden

The pattern of the gardens about the house is essentially geometric, with straight lines and chief features disposed about axes in harmony with the architecture of the house. This was a new idea of the Renaissance, scrupulously honoured today at Hatfield but enlivened by new planting which looks forward firmly to the future.

Montacute House

The influence of the Renaissance started later in England than in many other European countries, and lasted longer. Montacute House was built in the very last years of the sixteenth century, a house of palatial splendour rising in the rural landscape of south Somerset. It is built of the beautiful local stone from Ham Hill, a tawny, golden limestone which glows in sunlight and remains warmly attractive even when the sky is overcast. It has the symmetry of a Renaissance house, and some of the detailing—of pediments, gables and arches—but it is a very English house in that a certain severity underlies its decorative ebullience. The man who commissioned it was Sir Edward Phelips who came from a long established West Country family. He rose to prominence and wealth as a very successful lawyer, became a Member of Parliament and held official appointments under both Queen Elizabeth I and King James I. He also possessed a house in London and another country house at Wanstead in Essex, more conveniently placed for court life. On his death in 1614 his son Robert inherited and the Montacute estate remained in the family into the twentieth century, becoming the property of the National Trust in 1931.

From the moment it was built the wonderfully ornamental house has always been the focal point of the gardens. But long before this there had been a deer park, part of the monastic estate founded by Mortain who gave the land for the foundation of a Cluniac priory in the twelfth century. These lands eventually passed into the Phelips family whose new garden at Montacute is documented from quite early on. Gerard, writing in 1630, describes 'large and spacious Courtes, gardens, orchards, a parke.' The 'Courtes' referred to are walled enclosures, several of which survive today. Later in the seventeenth century a detailed survey describes these formal enclosures, giving much detail of their appearance. All this survived the eighteenth century fashion of landscaping, which often ran up to the very walls of the house. In the nineteenth century there are paintings and records of some of the planting carried out at that time. But the essential, and rare, charm of Montacute comes from the remarkable garden enclosures which survive from the early seventeenth century.

Clipped yews run around the
sunken lawn in the North Garden
with its central pool (above, right)

facing page

Wrought-iron gates
at the centre of the East Court

An urn at the entrance
to the North Garden

The East Court is one of the finest architectural ensembles of its period to survive in any British garden. Its surrounding walls are balustraded with coping punctuated at regular intervals by tall obelisks and airy stone lanterns. It is a rectangular space, closed on the corners furthest from the house by a pair of delightful gazebos. These, with their ogee roofs, elaborate parapets and small-paned leaded windows command views over the parkland to the east. In the 1667 survey they are described as '2 faire Turretts with lodging Chambers, all built with Freestone.' In Tudor gardens it was the tradition to provide vantage points overlooking deerparks so that the ladies could see the hunt in which they did not take part. These could well have served that purpose. Nothing is known of the planting in the East Court until the nineteenth century when the walls were lined with borders planted in ethereal shades of lilac, grey and white, sparked with bright yellow sunflowers and scarlet zinnias, as shown in G.S. Elgood's watercolour of 1886. In the 1950s these borders were replanted according to the designs of Phyllis Reiss who lived nearby at Tintinhull House. She laid out a bold and harmonious scheme —which survives today— of chiefly herbaceous perennials, in yellow, purples and the occasional flash of red. Golden yellow achilleas, rich purple linarias and blood-red penstemons spread out about repeated clumps of two purple-leafed shrubs, the smoke bush (*Cotinus coggygria* 'Royal Purple') and *Berberis thunbergii* 'Atropurpurea'. Beyond the walls of the court to the east an eighteenth century avenue of limes (*Tilia europaea*) draws the eye towards the countryside. On the far, western, side of the house a new approach to the house was added by Edward Phelips in 1785 with fine wrought-iron gates and gate piers on the road. A mixed avenue of cedars of Lebanon (*Cedrus libani* sbsp. *libani*), Irish yews (*Taxus baccata* 'Fastigiata') and beeches (*Fagus sylvatica*) leads up to the western façade of the house—in effect a continuation of the old lime avenue to the east. This has the effect of pinning the house down firmly in the landscape.

The North Garden, adjacent to the East Court, is called 'a very faire and Spacious Garden walled about and furnished with all sorts of Flowers' in the 1667 survey. It is sunken, at a lower level than the East Court, surrounded by raised walks. Rows of clipped Irish yews (*Taxus baccata* 'Fastigiata') and of the thorn *Crataegus lavallei* give powerful structure and at the centre of the court is a balustraded pool put

The facing sides of the East Court
with their symmetrical
architectural detailing

Detail of the finials which
run along the coping of the East
Court walls

into place in the late nineteenth century. Running below the south wall is a handsome border planned by Vita Sackville-West and Graham Stuart Thomas in the late 1940s. Both were deeply interested in old and species shrub roses, which at that time were unfashionable. Substantial species, like *R. glauca* and the Himalayan *R. moyesii,* are planted at the back of the border intermingled with garden forms known to have been in existence when Montacute House was built, such as the Jacobite rose, *R. alba* 'Alba Maxima'; in the middle of the border are smaller shrub roses which include several hybrid musk roses (like *R.* 'Princesse de Nassau') and Gallicas (like 'Cardinal de Richelieu' and 'Charles de Mills'). All these, deliciously scented in late June, are underplanted with waves of the glaucous-leafed *Hosta fortunei* var. *hyacintha*.

The exceptional architectural setting of Montacute has provided a framework for gardening of rare opportunities. Ingredients from different periods live harmoniously together linked by the underlying structure of architectural 'garden rooms'. These have sufficiently powerful character of their own to live happily with the later plantings, creating a delightful blending of styles.

The East Court pavilions
seen from outside

Montacute House Gardens

Montacute House

The east façade of Montacute
House seen from the Cedar Lawn

Penshurst Place

The east façade of the house
seen from the Union Flag Garden

'There is no finer or more complete fourteenth century manor house than Penshurst Place',
wrote Nikolaus Pevsner in *The Buildings of England*. It was built from 1341 onwards for Sir
John de Pulteney, an immensely rich London merchant. Sir John died without an heir and the
estate changed hands many times until it was acquired in 1552 by Sir William Sidney—it has
remained in the ownership of his descendants ever since. The house preserves magnificent rooms of
the fourteenth century and marvellous portraits of the Sidney family from the sixteenth century
onwards. The garden, too, is a most unusual survival from the past.

The setting of the house is memorably beautiful. To the north of the house and its walled garden is
a deer-park of Medieval origins—the Sidney oak (*Quercus robur*) may well date from this time—and
an avenue of limes (*Tilia europaea*) planted in the late seventeenth century to celebrate the accession to the throne of King William III. To the east and south the house looks out over a vast walled
garden, 10 acres (4 hectares) in area. This enclosure dates from the sixteenth century, built of the

The village church forms
an eyecatcher from the rose garden

slender bricks of the period, and the paths and division of space probably date from that period. At all events they have not changed in essence since Kip's engraving of c.1700 which shows a cruciform pattern of major axes within whose compartments sub-divisions are much as they remain today. By the nineteenth century the garden had decayed and a major restoration was undertaken by the architect George Devey in the 1850s. In the twentieth century parts of the garden were replanted to the designs of Lanning Roper and John Codrington. Despite these changes the old underlying pattern of the garden has remained, giving it harmony and structure.

The site is flat so that the house and the nearby tower of the village church of St John the Baptist are strong architectural reference points in the landscape. Immediately south of the house the Italian Garden retains the Victorian revivalist character established by George Devey. At the centre a spacious circular pool is embellished with a statue and fountain. It is surrounded by a parterre-like arrangement of lawns and box-edged beds planted with pink roses and to the north and west raised terrace walks give fine views of the patterned garden and of the gently undulating rural landscape beyond the garden walls to the south. On the east and south sides the Italian Garden is hedged in yew (*Taxus baccata*) with the top clipped into graceful humps. A gravel path leads east flanked with borders designed by Lanning Roper. Strongly shaped shrubs such as *Cotinus coggygria* Purpureus Group and *Juniperus pfitzeriana* 'Pfitzeriana' are underplanted with the spreading polyanthus rose 'The Fairy', *Alchemilla mollis* and *Stachys byzantina*. To the south a rose garden has standard roses underplanted with *Stachys byzantina* and a pair of remarkable seventeenth century polyhedral sundials. These most ornamental garden ornaments are often seen in old Scottish gardens but only rarely in England.

The Lanning Roper borders lead to the chief north-south axis of the garden which is dominated by a pair of herbaceous borders with daylilies (*Hemerocallis* cultivars) in shades of yellow and apricot, hardy geraniums, acanthus and phlox. These borders are backed by apple trees, for this is one of the chief fruit-growing areas of England. To the east there is an abrupt change of mood, from the exuberantly floriferous to the austerely formal. A simple grass path leads between hedges of clipped yew

left

The Union Flag Garden whose
colours are picked out in red
and white bedding roses
and blue lavender

The pool at the centre
of the Italian Garden

facing page

The parterre in the Italian Garden
with blocks of clipped box
and pink roses

Penshurst Place

against which, spaced at regular intervals, are tightly clipped mounds of golden yew (*Taxus bacca-ta* Aurea group). Decorative enclosures lie on either side of this passage. To the north is a garden of magnolias designed by John Codrington with, immediately behind it, the theatre garden with an amphitheatre of turf. To the south of all this is one of the handsomest and least expected features—a splendid orchard of apples, with many substantial specimens of 'Bramley' planted in state-ly rows with a grassy meadow at their feet and close-mown paths leading their way through the long grass. Adjacent to the orchard is a nut garden, with several varieties of another Kentish speciality, the hazelnut, or cobnut as it is called in Kent. In the far north-eastern cor-ner the Union Flag Garden has powerful nineteenth century character but Tudor gardens also had such emblematic schemes of cheerful colours. The pattern and colours of the flag are formed by red and white bedding roses and blue lavender (*Lavandula angustifolia* 'Munstead'). Variety and surprise are the chief qualities of Penshurst Place gardens. The harmonious pat-tern of paths, walls and hedges, with enticing vistas offered at every turn, makes it a most delightful garden to walk in. It is not one of those historic gardens which seem overburdened by the past. Indeed, its history provides the unostentatious background for the great variety of garden themes which are woven so sympathetically together.

left
___

In the herbaceous borders plants are allowed to stray into the gravel. The tower of the church of St John the Baptist forms a borrowed ornament in the garden

In the formal orchard close-mown paths make a firm pattern in the long grass

Penshurst Place

A double herbaceous border, which forms a principal north-south axis
in the garden, explodes into exuberance in high summer with drifts
of flowers softening the formality

Hampton Court Palace

Hampton Court Palace, in its idyllic setting on the banks of the river Thames south-west of London, is one of the most beautiful, and best preserved of the English royal houses. It also has a remarkable garden history, with features of different periods going back to the early sixteenth century when it was built. It was built during the reign of King Henry VIII for a Prince of the Church, Cardinal Wolsey, who had acquired the estate in 1515. It was in its day the greatest house in England, 300 x 559 feet in size, greater even than the Château de Chambord, the palace of Henry's great rival François I, by the banks of the Loire. A contemporary visitor, the Duke of Württemberg, described Hampton Court as 'the most splendid and most magnificent royal palace of any that may be found in England, or indeed in any other kingdom.' Cardinal Wolsey's power and plutocratic way of life threatened the status of the king, whom he attempted to appease by handing over the Hampton Court estate in 1525. It has remained in the ownership of the royal family ever since. At the end of the seventeenth century King William III made Hampton Court his chief palace which he greatly enlarged, to the designs of Sir Christopher Wren, to rival the palace of Louis XIV at Versailles. In the following century Hampton Court continued to be used as a royal palace until the death of King George II in 1760 after whom no monarch has lived there.

A drawing by Anthonis van Wyngaerde of the gardens at Hampton Court, among the earliest detailed pictures of any English garden, shows them in around 1555, shortly after the death of Henry VIII. To the south of the palace a series of walled gardens ran down towards the bank of the river. Two of the gardens were disposed in a pattern of square beds and one was ornamented with a large number of carved heraldic beasts mounted on poles. A contemporary bill survives—'For making bestes in tymber for the kynges new garden.' A triangular garden had a Mount, a raised hillock with a glass arbour surmounted by a lead cupola, from which views of the garden and of the Thames beyond the walls could be admired. Part of these gardens were built over in the late seventeenth century when Wren's spectacular new palace was added to the old. But surviving fragments include part of the walls of Henry VIII's Privy Garden and his Pond Garden, with a not entirely sympathetic modern bedding scheme of annuals.

At the end of the Privy Garden exquisite wrought-iron screens by the Huguenot craftsman Jean Tijoux frame views of the river Thames

The newly restored Privy Garden seen from the roof of the palace with
a detail of one of the statues below the windows of Sir Christopher
Wren's state appartments

After the restoration of the monarchy in 1660 King Charles II returned to England determined to make the sort of gardens he had seen in France during his exile at Saint-Germain-en-Laye. To the east of Christopher Wren's new palace a giant semi-circle of *parterres de broderie* was laid out leading to a *patte d'oie* of three avenues of lime trees (*Tilia europaea*). Further European influence came with King Charles's Dutch successor, William III, who came to the throne in 1688. He brought with him the French Huguenot designer Daniel Marot, who had worked in the Netherlands on the royal palace of Het Loo. A magnificent new Privy Garden was laid out between the Wren palace and the river, a sequence of elaborate parterres culminating in a exquisite screen of wrought-iron executed by another Frenchman, Jean Tijoux. A painting of 1702 by Leonard Knyff shows this scheme shortly after its completion. It is a clever design for a difficult site, because the river cuts across at an oblique angle to the façade of Wren's new palace. The area is essentially a rectangle, divided by paths into four with a central circular pool. Where it adjoins the river there is a circle of grass with a statue in the centre and Tijoux's screen curves elegantly about it, providing a harmonious finishing point.

The privy garden decayed in subsequent periods and by the late twentieth century it had become a lugubrious overgrown shrubbery, with no traces of its original decorative character, although among the trees were several yews almost 300-year-old, overgrown specimens of topiary from the old garden. The tercentenary of William III's accession to the throne was celebrated in 1988 and an exhibition was organised at Hampton Court Palace showing how the Privy Garden had appeared in its heyday. The restoration of the gardens at Het Loo between 1977 and 1984 was a pioneer venture in the meticulous reconstruction of gardens of this type. The combination of archaeological investigation, including an excavation of the site, together with the most detailed research into contemporary written accounts permitted a more accurate restoration than had ever been attempted before. In 1993 an excavation of the Privy Garden at Hampton Court Palace revealed, in the most precise detail, the outlines of *plates-bandes*, the sites of the plinths of statues and even the original drainage trenches. By 1996 the Privy Garden had been restored, looking resplendent spread out beneath the windows of Wren's palace. 2,500 yards of box hedging had been propagated to order from a specially chosen

Summer bedding schemes reflect the public character of parts of the garden

clone of *Buxus sempervirens* 'Suffruticosa' which was judged to be the closest to the original. The ornamental planting was chosen from plant lists contemporary with the original garden and thousands of plants were raised from seed for it.

Other parts of the garden at Hampton Court Palace also merit the kind of meticulous restoration which has so triumphantly brought the Privy Garden back to life. In particular the early sixteenth century gardens of Henry VIII and the French-style parterres of Charles II's time, both of which are overlaid by later changes, would be worthy candidates. In the twentieth century the gardens, freely open to the public, have assumed the character of a municipal park, rather than those of a royal palace. Brilliantly coloured summer bedding schemes were introduced to the delight of many visitors but to the great detriment of the true character of the place. If you stand with your back to Wren's addition to the palace and look south across the Privy Garden, with the Thames glittering beyond Tijoux's marvellous wrought-iron, you can experience the potential of skilful restoration. Similar magic worked in other parts of the garden could make it into one of the greatest of European gardens.

Bramham Park

At the turn of the seventeenth into the eighteenth century the overwhelming style of British gardens was formal, ultimately derived from Renaissance principles. The engravings of Johannes Kip in *Britannia Illustrata* (1707), which illustrate English country houses and their gardens, show this plainly. For the most part, these estates possessed fairly simple layouts of a provincial charm. Some, though, belonged to the greatest estates, in touch with fashionable ideas, such as Badminton in Gloucestershire. The engravings of this house and its surroundings show a grandiose layout, with vast patterns of avenues dividing the landscape, and immensely elaborate formal gardens framing the house. The Baroque garden in France had already influenced the greatest, usually royal, English estates but it had yet to spread more widely. Le Nôtre died in 1700 but his ideas had continuing currency in Britain through Antoine-Joseph Dezallier d'Argenville's book *La Théorie et la Pratique du jardinage* (1709) which appeared in English in 1712 and enjoyed much success. It appeared, anonymously, with the title *The Theory and Practice of Gardening* in a translation by John James. It ran through three editions in the first half of the eighteenth century and the subscription list shows that it was bought by some of the grandest landowners, among them John Aislabie at Studley Royal (see page 67).

Few of the gardens made at this time survive in anything resembling their original form. Many were destroyed in the craze for the informal landscape park which overtook the country in the course of the eighteenth century. Bramham Park is one of the most complete, and most attractive, to survive. The house at Bramham was started in around 1700 for Robert Benson, the first Lord Bingley (1676-1731), who was probably his own architect. Built of fine pale stone, its spectacular entrance courtyard is rather in the manner of a French *cour d'honneur*. Although most of the garden layout is on the far side of the house, the view from the courtyard already shows the scale of Benson's landscape ambitions. The stone gate-piers, ornamented with sphinxes and leopards, frame a view of the arrow-straight drive sweeping up and down over the undulating parkland and appearing to go on forever. Benson, who had travelled widely in France and Italy on the Grand Tour, seems also to have been his own designer for the gardens. It is a gigantic conception, covering no less than 250 hectares. Benson laid out its essential plan which was embellished, with ornamental buildings and other features, throughout the eighteenth century.

The south-west façade of the house looks across open ground with long avenues of trees animated in spring by sheets of narcissi.

From the entrance courtyard there are tantalizing views of the gardens framed by the colonnades that flank the house. The chief axis of the design, rather eccentrically, runs parallel to the south front of the house. Its north-western extremity is marked by an eye-catcher in the form of an elegant summer-house (later converted into a chapel) designed by the architect James Paine in about 1760. The axis then runs along a terrace below the façade of the house and descends to spectacular water gardens with a pool and cascades, forming a cross axis. Part of the pool points to the south-west where, on rising land, an octagonal Gothic temple stands out. Beyond the water garden the axis plunges into woods, rising and falling, leading towards the Round House: a colonnaded and domed Ionic temple, also dating from the middle years of the eighteenth century, which may well also be by James Paine. Beyond it, deep in the woods, rising from an avenue of Douglas firs (*Pseudotsuga menziesii*) is a soaring obelisk. This was erected by Benson's daughter Harriet Fox in memory of her young son Robert who died in 1768. The obelisk stands at the meeting place of a gigantic *patte d'oie* of ten avenues which radiate out into the woods know as Black Fen. These are only a part of a bewilderingly elaborate pattern of rides still to be found in the woods.

South-west of the house are the true pleasure gardens of the estate. Spread out immediately in front of the house is a formal rose garden with rows of Irish yews (*Taxus baccata* 'Fastigiata') laid out in 1906 and still preserving the atmosphere of that period. This was originally an eighteenth century parterre, perhaps a *parterre de broderie*, which was usually the style immediately alongside the house. The ground here slopes upwards and then it is cut away, with stone retaining walls and an elaborate formal rococo cascade at its south-westerly extremity. Above it, continuing the axis, an apron of grass pierces the woodland beyond —perhaps this was, in the eighteenth century, the beginning of a much longer vista aligned with the centre of the house.

On the slopes above the rose garden are a series of remarkable *allées* of beech (*Fagus sylvatica*) hedges and grass paths. In many places the hedges rise over 20 feet high and there are two miles of them. In summer they form cool green passages and in the winter they glow with the warmth of the colour of their russet leaves. But the pattern of the *allées* is haphazard, for they often veer off at an angle and sometimes they appear to have no particular destination. However, they are often aligned with ornaments or buildings of which views are suddenly opened out. Where they end at the boundary of the garden there is occasionally a kind of bastion, raised on a stone wall, from

Bramham Park

South and west of the house beech
allées quarter the land enlivened
with fine eyecatchers

which there are beautiful views of the landscape. Because it is difficult to 'read' the pattern it is remarkably easy to get lost, but there is always an element of surprise which is one of the most attractive qualities of the garden.

The most striking difference between the landscape at Bramham and that of a French formal garden is the playfulness of Bramham. It is true that Le Nôtre allows himself the occasional joke (such as the concealed canal at Vaux-le-Vicomte) but underlying his designs, wherever the lie of the land permitted it, there is always a sternly dominating pattern of symmetry. This does not exist at Bramham, where vistas shoot off in unexpected directions, a canal is shaped like a lop-sided T and marvellous views of the rural landscape are deliberately exposed at the ends of vistas. In all this, Bramham seems to be the entirely characteristic product of a particularly English taste for independence and genial improvisation.

Bramham Park

facing page

An early eighteenth century
urn at the meeting point
of four allées

top

The long vista south-east of
the house terminates in an obelisk

above

The Round House, possibly
designed by James Paine, dates
from the early eighteenth century

The GothicTemple, on rising land,
commands long views. It dates
from shortly after 1742

Bramham Park

The long straight drive runs
up to the entrance courtyard
which is embellished with
exquisite stonework ornament

James Paine's summer house, built
in about 1760, was later turned
into a chapel

The cascades of the water garden,
built in the French baroque style
between 1700 and 1710,
are superbly ornamented

The house and gardens at Kinross were designed for his own use by the architect Sir William Bruce. Bruce lived from 1630 to 1710 and was the most important architect of his day in Scotland, becoming Surveyor-general of the King's Works. During the Commonwealth he had supported the Royalist cause and was actively engaged in the campaign to restore the monarchy. He travelled to the Low Countries to visit the exiled King and it seems probable that he also visited France in the 1650s. He was certainly familiar with new ideas in garden design from France which he introduced to Scotland in a distinctive and delightful way.

The garden façade of the house
seen from the end
of the herbaceous borders

The estate lies on the edge of the town of Kinross, north-east of Edinburgh not far from the Firth of Forth. Bruce bought the land here in 1675, much attracted by the romantic lake, Loch Leven, with its ruined medieval castle on an island at its centre. He planned the garden and park before he started work on the designs for his house, which was not completed until 1693. The grand idea that lies behind his garden design is that of linking the chief axis of the garden with the high street of the town and with a distant eyecatcher, the ruined castle at the centre of the loch. This technique for linking a house and garden with its surrounding landscape was one that was familiar in French gardens. For example, at the Château de Balleroy in Normandy, designed by François Mansart and built between 1626 and 1636, the main street of the village forms an avenue leading to the château. At Versailles three avenues converge on the Place d'Armes and the central Avenue de Paris is, in effect, the beginning of the axis that is continued on the far side of the château with the Tapis Vert and the Grand Canal about which the chief ornamental ingredients of the gardens are disposed. In Scotland this way of locating a house in its landscape was unknown until William Bruce employed it.

left

The Fish Gate whose wrought-iron
gate give views of Loch Leven
with, on an island, the ruins
of Loch Leven Castle forming an
eyecatcher

The house and garden at Kinross survive today in a remarkably complete state. They are in private ownership and finely kept. Although the planting is entirely modern it is skilfully executed and takes excellent advantage of the site. The garden is walled on three sides with the house lying at the heart of the enclosure. The approach to the house from the lodges in the town is one of the grandest of any Scottish house, running arrow – out straight towards the long low house, dividing in front of a lawn that spreads below the windows of the house. On

above

The garden façade of the house

A late seventeenth century
urn in the flower garden

this side of the house there is little sign of a garden – grass, trees and the enclosing walls are all that may be seen. The garden proper lies on the far side of the house. Here the land slopes gently downwards towards the banks of the loch which is visible over the garden wall with gentle hills sweeping above its far banks. Immediately behind the house a deep gravel walk is marked at each end by a stone statue of a recumbent lion. From the walk, a path leads to a square enclosure hedged in yew (*Taxus baccata*) with a circular central lily pool with a lead swan in the middle. In each corner of the square are beds of roses arranged in blocks of a single colour—white (*Rosa* 'Korbin' Iceberg) and yellow (*R.* 'Arthur Bell'). At the centre of each bed rises a tall helical column of clipped yew. Broad, shallow steps lead down to a pair of herbaceous borders flanking the axis which leads towards the loch. The borders are backed with five-foot hedges of purple beech (*Fagus sylvatica* Atropurpurea Group) and the planting within them is arranged more or less as a mirror image on each side. The colours modulate gently from white (*Anthemis punctata* subsp. *cupaniana*, *Galega officinalis*, *Veronicastrim virginicum*) to purples and blues (*Salvia sclarea* var. *turkestanica*, *Geranium pratense* 'Plenum Violaceum', *Echinops ritro*) and ending in a brilliant fanfare of red *Persicaria affinis* and scarlet *Crocosmia* 'Lucifer'.

The focal point of the herbaceous borders, despite the floriferous fireworks on either side, is a gate let into the garden wall. A wrought-iron grill permits views of the ruins of Loch Leven Castle rising on its island in the loch. The castle, of romantic appearance, has romantic associations, for here Mary Queen of Scots was incarcerated in the sixteenth century. The gate is supported on finely carved piers surmounted by putti playing with dolphins and an stone arch with stone cornucopias runs over the

An ogee-roofed pavilion in the 'secret garden'

One of a pair of stone lions guarding the house

gate with, at its centre, a bowl of fish. The fish are beautifully carved and each species, of which there are seven, is identifiable – all were species to be found in the loch in the seventeenth century. On either side of the gate the garden walls spread out, regularly embellished with piers capped with stone lions or finials on the parapet. Deep herbaceous borders lining the walls are divided by buttresses of yew fitting in harmoniously with the strongly architectural setting.

The walls that enclose the garden are almost entirely lined with borders. But closer to the house the walls are interrupted by especially boldly carved and decorated piers which flank openings. On one side they lead to a path leading to a church ('kirk wynd') which no longer exists and on the other they exposed a view of an idyllic grove of trees. These were part of Bruce's original scheme and, once again, formed a link between the enclosed world of the garden and the greater landscape outside it. Close to the house, hard against its south-west corner, is a secret garden. Its chief ornament is an elegant garden pavilion, with a sweeping ogee-shaped roof of a characteristically seventeenth century Scottish style. It is one of a pair which end curving walls that extend outwards from the house and are visible on both sides of the wall. The secret garden is a lively arrangement of gravel paths, lawns and bedding roses with a fine lead statue of Atlas bearing the weight of the earth on his shoulder. The garden wall here is decorated with finials and a multifaceted sundial of a type frequently found in Scottish gardens of this period. The long hours of sunlight in these northern latitudes meant that a sundial with a single face was unable to show the time throughout the day.

Kinross is one of the most unusual and attractive historic gardens of the British Isles. Its greatest distinction comes from the rare quality of its architecture—house, walls and garden buildings—and its subtle but explicit relationship with its setting in the larger landscape.

Accidents of history can signal the start of remarkable gardens. The maker of the gardens at Levens Hall, Colonel James Grahme, enjoyed brief success as Privy Purse and Master of the King's Buckhounds to King James II who reigned from 1685 to 1688. Grahme, as a catholic, had no future under James's successor, the Dutch William of Orange, who became William III in 1688. Grahme long had connections with the north of England and, in 1689, bought from his cousin Alan Bellingham the ancient estate of Levens Hall in what was then Westmorland. Grahme remained in the south until Levens Hall had been altered to meet his needs. However, he meticulously directed works on his new estate and a remarkable collection of letters survives, from the very busy period between 1692 and 1695, in which his steward, Hugh James, describes everything being done under his supervision. A letter of 1st November 1694 gives news of a momentous event in the history of the garden, the arrival of Guillaume Beaumont to create a new garden. Little is known of this mysterious Frenchman except that he was working for Colonel Grahme at his estate in the south of England at Bagshot and that he had worked on the royal gardens at Hampton Court under King James II. A portrait of him painted in about 1700 still hangs at Levens Hall and is inscribed 'Monsieur Beaumont Gardener to King James II and Col. Jas. Grahme. He laid out the gardens at Hampton Court Palace and at Levens'. Although there is evidence of Beaumont at Hampton Court, and at other English gardens such as Longleat in Wiltshire and Forde Abbey in Dorset, nothing is known with any certainty about the work he carried out.

Some of the yew topiary is clipped into representational shapes – here a crown surmounts an archway

<u>above</u>
Old trees are allowed to remain among the topiary, adding their naturalistic character

<u>right</u>
A new parterre of pansies and clipped box

Wild garlic (*Allium ursinum*) grows
under the ancient beech hedges

Levens Hall

The earliest ha-ha in England, dating from 1695, and an avenue of sycamores across a pasture

The first house at Levens had been built in the thirteenth century and there had been a medieval deer-park. When Grahme bought the estate there were already avenues in place planted earlier in the seventeenth century. The garden that Beaumont laid out, however, was in an entirely new style, unlike anything that had been seen in this remote part of the country before and, in one respect, unlike anything else in the country of this date. Within days of his arrival Beaumont was hard at work on the new garden. Hugh James's letter of 12th November 1694 records that 'Mr Beamount [the spelling varies] begun to worke in the Garden this day sevennight, and is Levelling and Making the walke behinde the New building.' Subsequent letters trace the work, including the ploughing and levelling of the ground, the planting of 'greens' (i.e. evergreens, quite possibly yews for topiary) and the making of a substantial vegetable garden. James's last letter, written just before he died in April 1695, describes the work on 'the Ditch behind the Garden.' This was a ha-ha, or sunken fence, a garden device which already existed in France, but this is the first recorded use of it in England. In the following century, particularly in connection with the landscape park, it became an essential part of the vocabulary of English gardening.

54

Levens Hall

A watercolour plan of the newly made garden, dated 1730, still preserved at Levens Hall, is precious evidence of the original layout. To the south and east of the house he created a lively pattern of geometric beds embellished with yew topiary. A walk of beech (*Fagus sylvatica*) hedges was interrupted by a circular lawn linking it to a cross axis. The original planting survives, grown to vast size with dramatically gnarled trunks and beautifully underplanted with wild garlic (*Allium ursinum*). The essential layout, and much detail, of the seventeenth century layout, remains today — one of the most complete English gardens surviving from this date. Two factors have protected it from change. First, it has remained in private hands, passing only by descent since Colonel Grahme's death in 1730. Successive generations of the family have treasured the garden and ensured its survival. Secondly, this remote corner of England is essentially conservative and quite unconcerned with the fluctuations of metropolitan fashion.

The house at Levens is a fortified manor house, built at different periods from the thirteenth to the early eighteenth centuries. With its dramatic square tower it lies at the heart of the pleasure gardens. The gardens immediately to the east and north-east of the house maintain much of the character which Beaumont gave them. Much old yew topiary survives, now marvellously contorted with age. These became one of the most admired features, attracting visitors from far and wide. *Country Life*, in an article of 1899, described them — 'a peacock here, a huge umbrella-like construction there, an archway, a lion . . . and a host of other such adornments all shaped of ductile yew'. Some of these yew plants certainly date back to Beaumont's time but most are of much more recent date. Some of them, indeed, are of golden yew (*Taxus baccata* Aurea Group) which is unknown before the nineteenth century. For the underplanting of the topiary shapes seasonal bedding schemes are used. This tradition goes back to the nineteenth century when the head gardener, Mr Gibson, recommended the use of the tender *Salvia patens*—'the brilliant blue of flower against the dark green of the yew trees has a very striking effect indeed.' Two schemes are used today: in spring tulips are intermingled with violas and forget-me-nots; in summer brilliantly coloured verbenas are underplanted with such silver-leafed plants as *Helichrysum splendidum*.

The beech *allée* still forms the chief axis running south from the topiary garden. A cross axis to the west leads to the ha-ha with an avenue of sycamores (*Acer pseudoplatanus*) drawing the eye across parkland. West of the *allée* are quite new developments, among them a fine herb garden and a fountain garden created in 1994 to celebrate the tercentenary of Guillaume Beaumont's arrival at Levens. So, a lively horticultural continuity has been established in which the historic past provides an exceptional background for new gardening schemes.

Levens Hall

left

right

The white tulip 'Purissima' makes

the pansies in blocks of a single

a dazzling spring planting alongside

colour

57

In the topiary garden some of the yew plants go back to the original
late seventeenth century garden — their originally crisp outlines have
lost their definition after repeated clipping. New plants have been
added at various times subsequently, including golden yew
(*Taxus baccata* Aurea Group) which was unknown before the
nineteenth century

The original castle at Powis was built in the middle ages, occupying a defensive position in the county of Powys, quite close to the English border. The estate was bought in 1587 by Sir Edward Herbert who began to transform the castle into a house to live in, rather than merely a stronghold. Towards the end of the following century a spectacular new garden was made, taking every advantage of the precipitous slopes on the south side of the castle, and of the beautiful views. The most memorable feature of this new garden is the series of Italianate terraces which lie below the ramparts of the castle. No such complete scheme of this sort and date survives in any other garden in Britain. Their survival is little short of a miracle, for they endured neglect in the eighteenth century when the family lived elsewhere —and, as a contemporary writer recorded, 'horses grazed on the parterres'. In 1771 the landscaper William Emes was commissioned to make alterations to the estate, but plans to destroy the terraces— by blowing them up with gunpowder —and replace them with smooth turfed slopes in the style of the eighteenth century landscape park, never came to fruition.

It was William Herbert, the first Marquess of Powis, who created the terraced garden, starting in the 1680s. A little later, by 1705, an elaborate water parterre of thoroughly Baroque character had been laid out on flat ground at the foot of the terraced garden. It was described in a letter in that year from John Bridgeman: 'I din'd this week at Powis Castle. The water works and fountains that are fin-

The south façade of the castle, and the terracing, seen from the Wilderness

Fine early eighteenth century lead
figures ornament the balustrade
of the terraces from which
there are magnificent views to
the Breidden Hills

Powis Castle

ished there are much beyond anything I ever saw.' An engraving by Samuel and Nathaniel Buck printed in 1742 shows the result of these great works. The terraces are ornamented with walks of clipped trees and they descend to the water garden which is embellished with scalloped pools, statues and topiary. The Buck print shows a neat row of clipped trees running along the uppermost terrace. These could well be the original yew trees which today have formed giant rounded shapes, like green ramparts at the foot of the castle walls. An immense yew hedge, also quite conceivably dating from the original planting, now rising 30 feet high and magnificently billowing with age, marks the eastern end of the terraces.

In the early twentieth century a new formal garden was made on the site of the kitchen garden to the east of the castle which had originally been laid out by William Emes. In 1952 the estate was given to the National Trust in whose care the garden has flourished, giving full value to the surviving historic features but adding a distinctive style of planting, especially along the borders that line the terraces. These were replanted under the direction of Graham Stuart Thomas, Gardens Adviser to the National Trust, and they have changed gently from year to year. The bottom, or orangery, terrace has the deepest borders which are filled with chiefly herbaceous planting. Although harmony is given by repeated use of certain plants (for example the ethereal white veils of *Epilobium angustifolium* var. *album*) the essential effect is that of exuberant plantings of brilliant colours making a dazzling contrast with the stateliness and architectural detail of the terraces. The scarlet flowers of the tall *Crocosmia* 'Lucifer' rise among the rich golden apricot of *Alstroemeria aurea*; the rich red flowers and bronze foliage of the dahlia 'Bishop of Llandaff' are set off by the sprightly lemon yellow of *Achillea filipendulina* 'Gold Plate'; columns of sweet peas (*Lathyrus odorata*), trained on towers, soar above the planting—rich blue 'Lord Nelson' or sombre purple 'Matucana', both with exceptional scents. Occasional use is made of plants too tender to be thought of as perennials. The superb *Salvia guaranitica* from Brazil flaunts its deep blue flowers, reaching a height of six feet, at the back of the border. It is raised in pots from cuttings and put out in the spring when there is no further danger of frost. On the topmost terrace a whole bed is composed of tender plants grown in this way, giving a tropical luxuriance. Here are the giant leaves of *Tetrapanax papyrifer*, the rice-paper plant

View of the Great Lawn and
Formal Garden from the terraces

right and facing page above

The orangery built into the top
terrace with an eighteenth century
stone figure of Pan with his pipe

from Taiwan; the blues and scarlets of many tender species of *Salvia*; the soft orange plumes of the Canary Islands foxglove, *Isoplexis canariensis*; and the soft silver leaves of the Australian *Plectranthus argentatus*, with spikes of pale blue flowers. All this is a tribute to the skills of the gardening staff at Powis, who know how to make full use of the protected microclimate of the terraces with their south-eastern exposure.

The terraces are edged with stone balustrades ornamented with superb lead figures and statues dating from the early eighteenth century. A more recent introduction is the prolific use of pots, lavishly filled with skilful combinations of plants. These are placed at the top of piers or in the handsome pedimented niches of the castle walls themselves. The plants in the borders and pots continue to produce brilliant colour well into the autumn, bringing a celebratory lightheartedness to the severity of the castle.

Stretching out below the terraces is a great lawn – the site of the water parterres which were removed at the time of Emes's landscaping activities. Devoid of ornament, and closed on each side by a crisp hedge of yew, it provides a calm interlude between the grandeur of the castle and its floriferous fireworks and the Elysian character of the woodland garden that opens out on its far side. Here the land rises again, clad in shrubs and trees – this is the Wilderness, first planted by Emes in the late eighteenth century. Among superb oaks, both deciduous (*Quercus robur*) and evergreen (*Q. ilex*), and several splendid old yews, is a fine collection of specimen trees – with such species as *Koelreuteria paniculata*, *Liriodendron tulipifera* and *Davidia involucrata*. At the heart of the wood is a modern sculpture, a giant disembodied foot, carved in stone by Vincent Woropay, and resembling the last relic of some ancient and forgotten culture.

The garden at Powis is among the most attractive in Britain. Its masterstroke is to preserve the character of its best old features and enliven it with the relatively ephemeral planting of the terrace borders. The architecture – of buildings, hedges and topiary – provides the strongly decorative framework which permits such free and inventive planting.

above

The formal garden is enclosed in yew hedges with, to the south,
a wrought-iron gate supported by piers capped with griffins

Studley Royal

left

The ruins of the great Cistercian church of Fountains Abbey which form a visual climax to the garden

right and right above

The Gothic Octagon Tower on the wooded heights above the water garden. Originally built in classical style in 1728 and gothicised ten years later

John Aislabie, from an old Yorkshire family, inherited the Studley Royal estate in 1699. He was well connected both socially and culturally, being a friend of two of the most influential garden theorists of the early eighteenth century – Lord Burlington and Sir John Vanbrugh. He was also politically powerful, becoming Chancellor of the Exchequer in 1718. He embarked on a new garden at Studley Royal in 1716 choosing a site that was quite remote from his house, in the beautiful valley of the River Skell. Here he dammed the river, made a cascade and laid out immense expanses of formal pools – this gigantic task took ten years in all to complete and at times involved 100 labourers. Work was halted by the great financial scandal of the day, the South Sea Bubble. The South Sea Company had been founded as a company in South America trading chiefly in slaves. Its stock soared in value only to collapse dramatically in 1720. Aislabie was charged with 'a most dangerous and infamous Corruption' – he had himself speculated in the Company's shares, what we would call 'insider trading' today – and was imprisoned in the Tower of London. He was, however, released in 1723 and he retired permanently to his Yorkshire estates to lick his wounds and cultivate his garden.

By May 1729 he had repaid £2m (£100m in today's money) of his illicit South Sea profits. It gives some idea of the wealth that remained to him that his Yorkshire estates were untouched and he was able to spend vast sums on his garden and its exquisite buildings.

In his political exile John Aislabie poured all his energies into the garden at Studley Royal. The first part – a cascade and the geometric sweeps of water known as the Moon and Crescent Ponds – although formal, has none of the rigidity of, say, French and Dutch water gardens of the seventeenth century. Also, Aislabie's priceless advantage was the exquisite natural setting of which he took every advantage. The slopes were richly planted with beech (*Fagus sylvatica*), elm (*Ulmus procera*) and Scots pines (*Pinus sylvestris*) and the heights were embellished with splendid buildings. These served as ornaments in their own right, as places of retreat in which to meditate, as well as vantage points from which to admire the water gardens below. Some of these buildings no longer survive – a particular loss is the buildings in the Chinese taste described by visitors in the eighteenth century. Lord Burlington's circle collected pictures of Chinese gardens and garden features derived from them became fashionable, many of them sadly ephemeral. Philip Yorke visited Studley Royal in 1744 and described the valley with 'terraces interspersed with rock, which makes a Chinese landscape'. A painting of about 1760 by Balthasar Nebot shows an airy Chinese pagoda with a sweepingly curved roof commanding the heights above the valley.

The buildings that do survive are an integral part of the landscape. The Gothic Octagon Tower rises on a rocky crag high above the woods immediately to the east of the formal water gardens. It was built in 1728, in the classical style, but gothicised ten years later. From it there are views over the curved pools lying below and across the valley to a corresponding building among the trees on the far side of the valley. This is the Banqueting House, built between 1728 and 1732 to the designs of Colen Campbell. With its rusticated pilasters and arched windows it is a building of dashing elegance with an interior to match. It is a single room with apses at each end ornamented with beautifully carved decorations and fine plaster work. From the Banqueting House a panoramic view opens out to the south-east showing the whole formal water garden with the Temple of Piety at the very edge of the Moon Pool. The Temple of Piety, pillared in the Ionic style, was one of the last of the garden buildings to be completed before John Aislabie's death in 1742. From it there are fine views of the water garden and of the lead

above left
The early eighteenth century balustrading of the formal cascade of the water garden

above right
and facing page left
The Temple of Piety overlooking the Moon Pond with lead figures of Endymion and Neptune

The Banqueting House, built
between 1728 and 1732 to the
designs of Colen Campbell

figures of Neptune, Endymion and Bacchus that decorate its banks. The slopes that rise above
the Temple have been replanted in the way that Aislabie originally planned, with a naturalistic arrangement of yew, box, *Juniperus communis*, the sweetbriar rose (*Rosa eglanteria*) and the
Guelder rose (*Viburnum opulus*). These native, or anciently introduced, plants make a wild contrast with the classical temple nearby and the crisp geometry of the pools.

A modest little pavilion, Anne Boleyn's Seat, introduces the kind of scenic surprise that eighteenth century landscapers relished – the sudden revelation of the ruins of Fountains Abbey
on the banks of the river far below. Separated visually from the rest of the garden by a loop
in the river, this exquisite Cistercian abbey of the twelfth century had always been thought
of by Aislabie as the ultimate focal point of his garden. But it did not become part of the
estate until long after his death, when his son William bought it in 1768. Not only does this
great abbey provide a spectacular ornament in the landscape, exquisitely set on the banks of
the river, but it has special symbolic connotations for eighteenth century English landscapers.
The Gothic was thought to represent ancient domestic virtues, a traditional Englishness, to which
garden makers and politicians wanted to make an appeal. Almost every eighteenth century landscape garden has some neo-Gothic building. Only Studley Royal has the remains of a great Cistercian
abbey artfully worked into the layout of the garden.
The garden at Studley Royal shows the full evolution of English landscape taste from the water
garden, which looks simultaneously backwards to the Baroque and forwards to the naturalistic landscape park, and on to late eighteenth century picturesque taste in which a medieval building, with all
its romantic associations, dominates the landscape. William Aislabie himself continued his landscaping experiments on a virgin site nearby at Hackfall Wood. Here from 1750 onwards, on the dramatically precipitous slopes of the River Ure, he made a picturesque garden which survives today in sub-
lime dishevelment. So father and son in their lifetimes embraced the key developments in English garden taste in the eighteenth century.

The Moon and Crescent Ponds
and the Temple of Piety

The canal which runs past
the Moon and Crescent Ponds

A stone statue of Hercules and
Antaeus and a lead statue of the
struggling warriors by the banks
of the canal

below
The Moon Pond seen from the
Gothic Octagon Tower

Stowe

Stowe

above right

The Temple of Concord and Victory
(c.1748) facing down the Grecian
Valley

left

The Queen's Temple (c.1742)

A French visitor to Stowe in 1748 published a description of what he saw—'Enfin j'ai vu *Stow,* cette petite *merveille d*e nos jours, et le lieu le plus enchanté de toute *l'Angleterre.'* ('At last I have seen Stowe, this little marvel of our time, and the most enchanting place in the whole of England'). His book, *Les Charmes de Stow*, gives only the author's initials, J. de C., and his identity is unknown. But it is a remarkably early account by a foreign visitor to a garden that was a little later to fascinate the whole world of garden cognoscenti. The garden could only be regarded as 'small' in comparison with, say, Versailles, for it covers an area of 160 hectares and, even in the 1740s, was one of the largest gardens in England. The garden historian Christopher Hussey described Stowe as 'The outstanding monument of English landscape gardening'. It is outstanding because of the particular skills of the garden designers who worked there and because of the exceptional quality of the buildings and monuments that enliven the landscape. Its particular historical interest is that the transition from formality to naturalism is vividly displayed in a single setting. It was at Stowe that, in the words of Horace Walpole, William Kent the architect and garden designer 'first leapt the fence and saw that all nature was a garden'.

The estate was bought by the Temple family in the sixteenth century. Sir Richard Temple (later the first Viscount Cobham) inherited it from his father in 1697. South of the newly built house there were fine terraced gardens, with a central axis aligned on the parish church of Buckingham three miles away. From about 1711, having retired from the army, Temple was able to turn his attention to his estate and he embarked on a spectacular programme of architectural and garden-making activity. For the garden he consulted Charles Bridgeman, the pivotal figure in the transition from geometrical formality to a freer, more natural style. His architect, for the house and for garden buildings, was Sir John Vanbrugh, a central figure in the age of Baroque architecture and gardening. A bird's eye view by Bridgeman shows an essentially formal layout of radiating avenues and long vistas but, interspersed with these, are winding walks leading through woodland and there is no overall symmetrical layout. Much use was made of the sunken fence, or ha-ha, a French invention,

which kept livestock at bay but permitted uninterrupted views of the rural landscape – an essential feature of the naturalistic landscape park.

On Vanbrugh's death in 1726 Temple, now Lord Cobham, recruited James Gibbs as his architect. He designed various garden buildings but had no influence on the layout. The figure who was responsible for a major new departure in the character of the garden was William Kent. He started work in the late 1720s and created a wholly original style of garden, the Elysian Fields. He dammed a stream to make pools and cascades and planted the banks with trees, creating a naturalistic wood-land glade. Overlooking the valley, on an eminence, he placed the Temple of Ancient Virtue, a domed and colonnaded classical shrine containing sculptures of the great men of the ancient world – Homer, Socrates, Epaminondas and Lycurgus. On the far side of the stream he built the Temple of British Worthies, a curved arcade of golden stone with niches containing busts of Cobham's British heroes ranging from King Alfred, through Shakespeare to some of Cobham's admired contemporaries like the poet Alexander Pope. Here, as elsewhere in the garden, there is a political agenda lurking behind the garden buildings. The British Worthies are all congenial to one, like Cobham, who was Whiggish, protestant and firmly patriotic and their busts bear inscriptions which emphasise this. The bust of Queen Elizabeth I, for example, has the following words: 'She confounded the Projects and destroyed the Designs of Spain... took off the yoke of ecclesiastical tyranny, restored religion from the corruption of Popery.' Although these inscriptions are frequent-ly witty they are not frivolous, for these were serious matters.

To the east of Kent's Elysium Hawkwell Field was developed in the 1740s as a *ferme ornée*, an orna-mental farm with sheep grazing about the walls of a Gothic temple. On lower ground below Hawkwell Field the Upper River is spanned by Gibbs's Palladian Bridge, an arcaded covered build-ing of 1738, inspired by Palladio's design in his *Quattro Libri*. Its classical elegance makes a piquant contrast with the rural scene above and its Gothic temple.

In 1741 Capability Brown was appointed Head Gardener at Stowe – he was only 25 and this was his first major job. By 1747 he had laid out the Grecian Valley, just north of Hawkwell Field, using already the characteristic Brownian ingredients of shorn turf and subtly undulating belts of trees. Elsewhere in the garden he undid the formality of Bridgeman's designs, opening out vistas, and planting many new trees, in particular elm (*Ulmus procera*), beech (*Fagus sylvatica*) and Scots pines (*Pinus sylvestris*).

In its day Stowe was the most widely admired and visited garden in England. It was the first garden to which a guide-book was published, in 1744. But by the early nineteenth century much of its

The Palladian Bridge (c.1737)
in its semi-rural setting

original impetus had been lost and taste was changing. When the German garden connoisseur Prince Pückler-Muskau visited in 1826 he wrote 'The grounds were laid out long ago and are so overloaded with temples and buildings that the greatest improvement would be the pulling down of ten or a dozen of them.'

The estate languished throughout the nineteenth century and in 1921 it was sold, dispersing the priceless contents of the house and many of the precious statues and other garden ornaments which in many cases had been created for the garden. The house became a school which took great pains to maintain the gardens, but it proved a task beyond its means. In 1989 the gardens were taken over by the National Trust which has undertaken a vast and meticulous programme of restoration. Today it may be seen in better state than at any time since its eighteenth century hey-day, one of the most marvellous and attractive gardens in the country.

above and right

William Kent's Temple of British Worthies (c.1734) facing
across the Elysian Fields to the Temple of Ancient Virtue

Urn in a niche decorating the
façade of the Queen's Temple

above

The Chinese House built
in 1738 possibly to the designs
of William Kent

left

The interior of the Palladian Bridge

Stourhead

In 1769 a traveller, John Parnell, visited the new gardens at Stourhead and recorded that it was 'the most delightful Scene almost I ever beheld.' Visitors to the garden today may see more or less what Parnell saw over two hundred years ago and many of them have a similar reaction. It has a magical quality, unlike any other English garden of its period, that is remarkably seductive.

The garden's creator was one of those eighteenth century gentleman landscapers, Henry Hoare II, gripped by a passion for the new way of gardening, intent on making a garden for himself. He came from a banking family, whose private family firm still flourishes, and his father had commissioned a splendid mansion at Stourhead in the fashionable Palladian style from the architect Colen Campbell. Henry Hoare II, on his return from the Grand Tour in 1741, inherited his father's estate. Sometime after 1745 he started work on his garden. The site, a little distance from the house, was a handsome valley with a small river, the Stour, and a chain of ponds. He dammed the river and made a large irregular lake which was the centrepiece of his garden. He planted trees on the slopes above the lake and commissioned ornamental buildings, mostly designed by the architect Henry Flitcroft.

left and facing page

The Temple of Flora, facing west across the lake, was built in 1744

The overwhelming impression of Stourhead is that of a series of exquisitely framed views. A circuit walk girdles the lake from which there are Arcadian views across the water with buildings rising among trees. From time to time paths lead up the slopes, guiding the visitor to some building or a vantage point from which to relish some especially beautiful view. Because of the irregularity of the lake's shape, the paths offering different viewpoints and the variety of ornaments to be admired, the permutation of pleasures is almost infinite. There have been attempts, largely unsuccessful, to establish parallels between the layout and monuments of Stourhead and the journeys of Aeneas and the founding of Rome as described by Virgil in the *Aeneid*. Whatever may be the truth of that, there certainly are classical references at Stourhead whose meaning would have been plain to any educated eighteenth century visitor. The Pantheon, for example, the splendid domed temple which occupies a key position on the far side of the lake from the entrance to the garden, would certainly have evoked the classical Pantheon, built by Agrippa for the Emperor Augustus. At Stourhead it may be glimpsed from almost any part of the circuit walk about the lake. In a great chamber beneath the dome are statues of Diana, Ceres, Isis and Hercules, all of whom had associations with nature or gardens.

The first building which visitors encounter on their walk about the lake is the little pedimented and columned Temple of Flora which bears the inscription 'Procul, o procul este profani', from the *Aeneid*. 'Be gone, be gone, you who are not believers' may simply be an injunction to those unwilling to succumb to the floral charms of the place to keep out. To the south of the Temple of Flora, on the slopes high above the lake is the splendid Temple of Apollo on a wooded eminence. Apollo was associated with the Palatine hill in Rome and was, of course, the god of sun, with a preeminent significance for gardens – hence the placing of this Temple in a southerly position.

A building which also has classical resonance is the subterranean grotto at the western extremity of the lake. The grotto became a key ingredient of the eighteenth century landscape garden in England. Here at Stourhead it is given drama by the way it is approached: one moment you are walking along in the sun, the next you are plunged underground in the shivery gloom. John Britton, a visitor in 1801, perfectly caught its character: 'It will be impossible for me to describe the awful sensations which I experienced on entering its gloomy cells; my fancy was set afloat on a sea of conjecture.' The grotto has two sculptures, a reclining

The Temple of Flora

water nymph and a river god, deity of the River Stour, holding an urn from which the river flows, bearing the melancholy lines 'This stream, like Time, still hastens from my Urn / For ever rolling, never to return.' A hole in the wall of the grotto gives one of the most beautiful views of the garden, framing the Temple of Flora on the far side of the lake. It is these irresistible composed views, so close in spirit to the paintings of Claude, that for many visitors will be the most unforgettable memory of Stourhead.

Eighteenth century engravings of the garden show it in its infancy. The newly planted trees are still youthful and the close-clipped grass runs down to the very banks of the lake. The various garden buildings stand much more prominently than they do today, unencumbered by the mature plantings that now surround them. Since the eighteenth century, generations of the Hoare family have cared for the garden and added their stamp. In the nineteenth century many rhododendrons were added and they now make a brilliant splash of spring colour by the waters of the lake. Some visitors consider that such bright colours are inappropriate to the eighteenth century idea of a garden of water, grass, trees and architectural interludes. However, the essential character of Stourhead seems to have survived intact and its powers of enchantment may be experienced by any visitor. No garden, particularly a landscape garden which depends on trees, can continue unchanged – change is part of its nature. One major change has a bearing on the way the garden is perceived by visitors. In its eighteenth century heyday the approach to the garden was across lawns by the house. The valley, with the sparkling waters of the lake folded in the wooded slopes and animated by delightful buildings, was then revealed spread out below. It made a romantic and naturalistic contrast with the crisp Palladianism of the house. However, carparking demanded a new entrance for the thousands who visit it, and the view they enjoy on entering is no less beautiful, though it is slightly deprived of surprise and of meaning.

The Pantheon on a misty
autumn day with a fine beech
in the foreground

Bowood

The landscape designs of Capability Brown, and those of his followers, dominated English garden taste in the second half of the eighteenth century. This naturalistic style depends on the subtle disposition of groups of trees, expanses of water, shorn turf and the occasional ornamental building or cascade. Many drama critics have noted that the greatest actors are the least conspicuous, and the most economical in their effects – the same is true of best garden designers. Capability Brown's work, indeed, is often thought of, not as designed landscape but, simply, as the *beau idéal* of English rural scenery – nature rather than gardening. Bowood is one of Brown's best surviving designs and an admirable example of his distinctive style. However, there is more to the gardens than its Elysian eighteenth century park. For in both the nineteenth and twentieth centuries admirable new ingredients have been added to this many-layered landscape.

The estate at Bowood is an ancient one – part of it was a royal hunting ground in the middle ages. Its essential garden history starts in 1754 when it was bought by the first Earl of Shelburne whose son, later the first Marquess of Lansdowne, commissioned the architect Robert Adam to enlarge and embellish the existing house. Capability Brown was first consulted about designing the grounds in 1757 and work started in 1761. In the valley to the east of the house he dammed two streams to form a long, narrow and sinuous lake which, when the surface of the water is ruffled by a breeze, is easy to mistake for a river. Brown planted belts of trees, a characteristic device, to embellish the

Robert Adam's Mausoleum was built c.1762

above

The Doric Temple
(early nineteenth century)
on the south bank of the lake

above

The Doric Temple
(early nineteenth century)
on the south bank of the lake

below

The interior of the Mausoleum

boundaries of the estate. On the far side of the house a mausoleum, in honour of the first Earl Shelburne, was built in 1761 to the designs of Robert Adam, and Brown laid out much of the woodland planting in this area. He also devised two new drives to the house, an important consideration in the 18th-century landscape park. Drives served two purposes, apart from the obvious one of leading to the house. The way in which the house was revealed to visitors, and the way in which the new beauties of the landscape were displayed, were both vital aspects of the design.

A little later than Brown's work, in about 1785, a spectacular cascade was added in the woods to the north of the lake. It was designed by the Hon. Charles Hamilton, the creator of an outstanding and idiosyncratic landscape park at Painshill in Surrey. Associated with the cascade are man-made rocky cliffs, incorporating grottoes designed by Josiah Lane, the leading grotto maker of the day who had worked at Painshill, Stourhead (see page 78), Wardour Castle and other gardens. The cascade is well hidden in woods, the sound of its unseen waters leading the visitor to it. Nearby, Hamilton and Lane also made a hermit's cave ornamented with outcrops of tufa, and with stalactites and ammonites set into the ceiling. From the opening of the cave are idyllic views over the waters of the lake. An early nineteenth century Doric temple, previously in the pleasure grounds near the house, was moved in 1864 to the east bank of the lake where, half veiled in trees and rising on a grassy promontory, it makes a fine ornament.

When the great garden writer John Claudius Loudon visited Bowood in 1838 he commented on the many 'foreign trees planted by the first Marquess' among which were especially large tulip trees (*Liriodendron tulipifera*). The tree-planting continued under the third Marquess (1780-1863), under whom the garden was extended in the nineteenth century. In 1848-9 he planted a pinetum which, though suffering much storm damage, survives today and has been much added to in recent years. He first planted rhododendrons at Bowood in 1854, a tradition that has been kept up by subsequent generations. The collection has been much extended by the present Lord Shelburne and may be seen in the beautiful setting of old woodland of oaks and beeches at some distance south-west of the house. It is a superb undulating site, laced with walks, with great numbers of rhododendrons – both flamboyant cultivars (such as the 'Loderi' hybrids) and species such as *R. sinogrande*. At its highest point, Adam's mausoleum, the only ornamental building in the woods, makes a superlative centrepiece. It is both an essential part of the design of the woodland gardens, and it is linked visually with the distant house. A gap in the trees reveals immense views of the countryside with Bowood House at its centre. Equally, from the house, the mausoleum forms a memorable sight, especially when illuminated by the morning sun, rising among distant trees.

The third Marquess was also responsible for adding the parterres to the south of the house which preserve their Victorian character today. They are in the form of two long terraces, the upper of which was designed by Sir Robert Smirke in 1818 and the lower, by George Kennedy, in 1851. The upper terrace has two round fountain-pools and clipped Irish yews rising above a pattern of box-edged beds with bedding roses. It is spread out beneath the windows of an eighteenth century orangery whose walls are embellished with finely trained climbing plants – many roses, the ornamental vine *Vitis coignetiae* and *Fremontodendron californicum*. Steps guarded by lead figures of stags lead down to the lower terrace which is a simpler arrangement of lawns, beds of Hybrid Tea roses and an avenue of Irish yews. The western end of the lower terrace has an elaborate double staircase embracing a pool. Although there have been many changes in the detail of the planting in the terraces, their essential character of lively ornamentation is much as is seen in a water-colour of about 1857 by E. Adveno Brooks.

In 1955 the Marquess of Landsdowne decided that the only way in which he could afford to maintain the Bowood estate, with its park and gardens, was to reduce the cost of maintenance by demolishing the 'Big House.' This he did, leaving the beautiful ancillary buildings as a much reduced house. It was a drastic solution to a problem that bedevils many other estates. Bowood today, with its beautifully maintained gardens, presents an appearance of health and vigour.

The Lower Terrace was completed in 1851 to the designs of George Kennedy; the cascade was made c.1785 to the designs of the Hon. Charles Hamilton; in the informal gardens that surround the Mausoleum rhododendrons are grown in naturalistic style underplanted with sheets of bluebells

left

Josiah Lane's grotto, which
overlooks the lake, was made
in the 1780s

Old oaks and beeches form
the background for plantings
of rhododendrons in
the Mausoleum garden

Caerhays Castle

John Nash's Caerhays Castle dates from c.1808

The castle at Caerhays occupies a dramatic and beautiful position and its architecture, too, has more than a touch of drama. It was built in the early nineteenth century for John Trevanion to the designs of John Nash whose particular gift was for architecture of exotic style. This was by no means the first house on this remarkable site, for the estate had belonged to a great West Country family, the Arundells, but it passed in the fourteenth century by marriage to the Trevanions. John Nash did much work for the royal family, including the remarkable remodelling of Brighton Pavilion in a beguiling Orientalist style. At Caerhays he had a site of unusual beauty, at the opening of a valley on rising land facing south over the sea at Porthluney Bay. It is very easy to regard the fantasy castle he contrived as a giant ornament for the landscape rather than merely a house to live in.

Nothing is known of the early garden history of Caerhays. A persistent rumour associates Humphry Repton with the landscape here, but no documentary evidence supports it. Repton had, in fact, worked in association with Nash, designing the setting for Nash's houses, but this association had ended in 1802. The natural site would certainly have appealed to Nash as the perfect setting for the picturesque castle he designed. Furthermore, perhaps the Trevanions felt that they had already spent enough money on their new house and were unable to bear the costs of landscaping. The scale of the work on the new castle alone at Caerhays was so enormous that the expense depleted the resources of the Trevanions and in 1854 the estate was sold to Michael Williams, a Cornish mine owner, in whose family it remains today. Michael Williams's grandson, John Charles Williams, was

The castle faces down a shallow
valley towards the beautiful
Porthluney Cove

the man who gave the garden its essential character. He was one of an exceptionally distinguished group of gentleman plant collectors who started to build up unique collections of plants in the nineteenth century. They realised that Cornwall provided a climate, unique to England, in which the great Asiatic flowering shrubs – camellias, magnolias and rhododendrons – would flourish as almost nowhere else. The acid soil, often deep and fertile, also provided the perfect conditions for these plants. These Cornish gardens received many of the first introductions of Asiatic exotics, countless examples of which survive as outstanding specimens of their species. The south coast of Cornwall, warmed by the effects of the Gulf stream currents, has remarkably mild winters and, in addition, very high rainfall. The finest gardens of this sort are all on the south coast – the north coast of Cornwall, facing west into the teeth of the fiercest winds, has a very different climate. Furthermore, many of the south-coast gardens have been made in sheltered valleys or in bays affording protection from the prevailing wind.

J. C. Williams started his collection in the last years of the nineteenth century. From 1897 until 1934, just before his death, he kept a garden journal which recorded the immense numbers of plants added to his collection. From 1900 Williams became a patron of the expeditions of E.H.Wilson, one of the greatest plant-hunters of the day, who discovered over 3,000 new plants, mostly in the Hupeh and Szechuan provinces of China. A little later, Williams supported the expeditions of George Forrest, another exceptional plant-hunter in China, from whom seed flowed to Cornwall. Williams had the collector's notes describing the sites of the plants in the wild, which he used to try and find something equivalent at Caerhays. This necessarily involved much experimentation and the garden evolved as a kind of horticultural testbed. Thus, it was the plants rather than the gardener that chose their positions. Plants survived where they would grow best, not according to any aesthetic scheme.

But the lie of the land, and the jungle-like exuberance of the planting, chiefly on the gentle slopes above the castle, is very beautiful. Paths wind through woodland, which includes magnificent old beeches (*Fagus sylvatica*) which go back to the early nineteenth century, and startling groves of exotic shrubs, or superb single specimens, reveal themselves in stately progression. The range of plants grown is enormous and exceptional specimens of rarities are to be seen at every turn. These exotics are underplanted with swathes of the native species so abundant in these parts in seasons – bluebells (*Hyacinthus non-scripta*), wood anemones (*Anemone nemorosa*), primroses (*Primula vulgaris*) and wild garlic (*Allium ursinum*) – forming a charmingly simple counterpart to the rarities.

The Williams family, apart from their plant collecting activities, also embarked on energetic programmes of plant breeding. The first plants they took an interest in were narcissus species. But later they embarked on two genera with which they became particularly associated. They crossed *Camellia japonica* with the very early flowering *C. saluenensis* to form the hybrid *C. williamsii* from which many excellent cultivars were derived, including the beautiful pale pink 'Donation'. Rhododendrons have also been a longstanding interest at Caerhays. One of E.H.Wilson's most beautiful introductions, from Szechwan, was named *Rhododendron williamsianum* after J.C. Williams. Among the most successful rhododendrons bred at Caerhays have been the smaller evergreens such as *R*. 'Blue Tit' Group and *R*. 'Humming Bird' Group.

The garden at Caerhays is a fusion of different tendencies in English gardening. It is not a garden which has been designed in the sense that landscape architects would recognise. It is in essence a naturalistic garden but, because it gathers together plants from many different ecologies, it is quite unlike anything that may be seen in nature. It would be true to regard it primarily as a plant collection but the collection is disposed in a way that is sympathetic to the beauties of the natural landscape. The love of plants, and the desire to know and study them, is allied to a love of landscape. Some of the effects are perhaps unpremeditated but anyone who has seen the giant *Magnolia campbellii*, now over 70 feet high, flaunting its vivid pink flowers on a sunny March day alongside the castellations and ramparts of Nash's castle, must agree that they provide a marvellous sight.

Caerhays Castle

Caerhays Castle

The fallen petals of camellias
carpet a shady path

Caerhays Castle

(from top to bottom)

Rhododendron williamsianum;

Rhododendron campylocarpum;

tree ferns (*Dicksonia antarctica*);

Rhododendron sinogrande

Tresco Abbey

The Lighthouse Walk forms the
principal axis uniting the terraces

At the top of the Lighthouse Walk
is a figure of Neptune - part
of a ship's figurehead taken from
a wreck in 1841

The gardens at Tresco are the result of an encounter
between a remarkable man and an exceptionally
unusual microclimate. Tresco is one of the Isles of
Scilly, an archipelago in the Atlantic 30 miles off the
south-west coast of England. The climate is strongly
affected by the Gulf Stream current, so that frosts are
rare. Although the rainfall is not high the air is
humidified by the surrounding sea, greatly increasing
the range of plants that will flourish here. The man
who made the gardens was Augustus Smith, who
came to Tresco in 1834. The islands are part of the
Duchy of Cornwall Estate, a hereditary possession of
the Princes of Wales. Smith took a lease on all the
islands of which he became the Lord Proprietor.
Tresco is one of the most anciently inhabited of the
Isles of Scilly and a monastic community had lived
here as early as the sixth century and in the twelfth
century Benedictine monks built a priory whose
handsome ruins are still an ornament of the island.
Smith built a new house above the priory and set
about creating a garden to take advantage of the marvellous climate – but his chief obstacle was the vio-
lent Atlantic north-westerly winds. Around the ruins

of the priory he built walled enclosures which survive today and are one of the most atmospheric parts of the garden. He introduced many tender plants, especially those from the southern hemisphere, which had never been grown in Europe before. As early as 1850 the garden was already attracting admiring visitors. Augustus died in 1872 and was succeeded by his nephew Algernon. He had the idea of greatly extending the scope of the garden and created substantial shelter belts of trees, in particular Monterey pines (*Pinus radiata*) and Monterey cypress (*Cupressus macrocarpa*) and oaks (*Quercus ilex*). The first two of these were especially appropriate, for they are native to the coast of California and well adapted to the punishing salt-laden winds.

By the time Augustus Smith died in 1872 an unique garden had been created to which subsequent members of the family (now called Dorrien Smith) have immensely added. In January 1987 there was the coldest weather in the history of the garden, with below-freezing temperatures lasting for days causing many plants to be killed. A second blow was the great storm which afflicted the south-west of England in 1990 which caused a great deal of damage at Tresco, especially to the larger and older trees. But a remarkable recovery has been made and modern visitors will see little evidence of those afflictions.

The most ingenious aspect of Augustus Smith's original layout was the sequence of south-facing terraces he built, linked by steps. This imposes a strong pattern and opens up fine vistas both along the terraces and up or down the vertiginous flights of steps. Some plantsman's gardens, especially those of such exotic luxuriance as Tresco, can seem claustrophobic. Here, open, long views repeatedly present themselves, and from the topmost terrace there is a feeling of airy spaciousness, with beautiful views of the sea. Furthermore, various buildings and ornaments provide crisp shapes among the abundant vegetation. Augustus Smith built the delightful Valhalla in which is housed a collection of decorative figureheads from the ships wrecked in these dangerous. The ruined walls and Gothic arch of the priory ruins make a distinguished background to the lavish planting among them. A carved figure of Gaia by David Wynne, and a dramatic bust of Neptune at the head of the steps leading up from Lighthouse Walk provide decorative interludes in the press of foliage.

left

Part of the collection of figureheads preserved in Valhalla

above

the ruins of the Benedictine St Nicholas Priory date from the early twelth century

Within the framework of terraces and paths the planting is lavishly informal, rising in ramparts of foliage or spilling over onto paths. Although naturalistic in style the garden possesses groups of plants never seen together in nature. The sweetly scented honey spurge (*Euphorbia mellifera*) and the spectacular purple-flowered (*Geranium maderense*), both endemic to Madeira, seed themselves in many parts of the garden and are found among plants from Australasia or South America. Substantial trees – several different palms, species of *Metrosideros* from New Zealand, many wattles (*Acacia* species) and gums (*Eucalyptus* species) from Australia – provide dramatic large scale planting and also add further protection from the wind. Very large groups of shrubs and small trees include representative collections of several genera. From Australasia there is an immense number of species of *Olearia* (including the attractive natural hybrid which appeared at Tresco, *O. scilloniensis*) and of leptospermums; many cistus (chiefly from southern Europe); leucadendrons from South Africa (among them the beautiful silver tree, *L. argenteum*); melaleucas (and other genera of the myrtle family) from Australia; and a vast and fascinating collection of species pelargoniums, a South African endemic. A wide range of succulents include aeoniums (chiefly from the Atlantic Islands such as Madeira); superb agaves from Central America and California; and opuntias and yuccas from the southern U.S.A. and central America. Because of the humidity of the air it is possible to cultivate a good range of ferns, especially at the lowest level of the garden closest to the sea – tree ferns

(*Cyathea* and *Dicksonia* species) from Australasia, species and cultivars of such European natives as *Asplenium* and *Athyrium*, and *Woodwardia radicans* from south-east Europe. Countless bulbous plants provide brilliant splashes of colour throughout the year – the southern European *Scilla peruviana*, species tulips from the near-east, brilliant tritonias from South Africa and sprekelias from Mexico.

There can be very few gardens in the world that cultivate such an astonishing range of plants in the open as Tresco does. Few visitors, however knowledgeable, will be familiar with all the plants that may be seen, but the effect is far from being a discordant jumble. Augustus Smith's bold and well-conceived original layout, gently modified by subsequent members of the family, provides a framework of visual order. Furthermore, a deeper harmony comes from the fact that the plants, whatever countries they may come from, have in common the same growing conditions. So many of the plants come from islands or coastal regions sharing a similar climate to that of Tresco. Many gardeners have had the experience of juxtaposing two plants, finding the result unsatisfactory, and realising that the plants come from completely different ecologies. Such plants will not only fail to thrive but they will, as often as not, always look wrong.

above

The beautiful silver tree,
Leucandendron argenteum,
from South Africa

right

The spectacular flower of *Protea
lapidocarpodendron* from
South Africa

The figure of Neptune at the top
of the Lighthouse Walk

Tresco Abbey

Strong foliage shapes, such as the
giant toothed arms of *Agave
americana* and the shining almost
black purple of *Aeonium arboreum
atropurpureum*, create firm points
of definition in the mass of exotic
planting. Repeated, often self-
sown plants, like the purple
Geranium maderense also give unity

The Madeiran cranesbill
(*Geranium maderense*)
is naturalised at Tresco

Waddesdon Manor is in an especially beautiful part of Buckinghamshire, on rising land over-looking the vale of Aylesbury. The land here was bought from the Duke of Marlborough in 1874 by Baron Ferdinand de Rothschild, one of several members of his family to establish themselves in the county and to make remarkable houses. The architect at Waddesdon was a Frenchman, Hippolyte Destailleur, who designed a palace in which he wove together a kind of anthology of French renaissance architectural styles to create a fantasy Loire château built in lovely honey-coloured Bath stone. The interior is also a kind of anthology, but here much of the material is original, exquisite *boiseries*, ceilings and fireplaces from French houses chiefly of the eighteenth century many of which were destroyed by Haussmann's reconstruc-tion of Paris. Baron Ferdinand was a collector of the finest French decorative arts, and the house he commissioned formed the perfect setting for them.

In the matter of the gardens Baron Ferdinand's taste extended, again, to French examples. He chose the Parisian landscape architect Elie Lainé who devised in essence the layout that may be seen today. Baron Ferdinand left an account of the making of Waddesdon in his book *The Red Book* which records that Lainé was 'bidden to make designs for the terraces, the principle roads and plantations'. But Baron Ferdinand goes on to say that the detailed planting of 'the pleasure grounds and gardens were laid out by my bailiff and gardener according to my notions and under my superintendence.' The estate was farmland when he started and the site chosen for the house, the top of Lodge Hill, needed to be levelled for the house and its surrounding formal gardens. The slopes below were plant-ed with many trees, some of which were mature specimens moved into position by carts drawn by Percheron horses brought over from Normandy. A contemporary description survives of a tree being

An avenue of oaks leads to
the entrance of Waddesdon Manor

The terrace with its elaborate display of bedding with (right)
an experimental bedding scheme designed by the artist John Hubbard
for the millennium

An eighteenth century Italian
sculpture of Minerva and Tritons
reclines among rocks and ferns in
the aviary

moved from the village of Haddenham, some miles to the south of Waddesdon: 'It was an enthralling sight to see a beautiful tree drawn along our village street by some twenty horses in team.' These trees give the slopes of Lodge Hill much of the beauty and character they have to this day.

The carriage drives winding about the contours of the hill met at a roundabout north of the house marked by a pool and fountains with eighteenth century sculptures of Triton and nereids. These are the work of Giuliano Mozani and were made for the Duke of Parma's palace at Corlorno. Standing out against the shrubs that line the roundabout are white marble terms representing the seasons. This stately scene provides a calm arrival point for the visitor, which contrasts with the excitement and drama of the great house, now visible to the south, at the end of an avenue of oaks (*Quercus robur* and *Q. cerris*). Behind the trees to the west is an enchanting rococo aviary of delicate filigree work and providing a home for a large collection of exotic birds. The central pavilion, from which curving wings extend, is embellished with a grotto-like arrangement of ferns and pool with an eighteenth century Italian statue of Minerva accompanied by frolicking tritons. A lawn is edged with beds containing massed plantings of white roses (*Rosa* 'Korbin' Iceberg) and the whole is enclosed with yew hedges.

The grand simplicity of the approach to the entrance front of the house contrasts with the drama at the front façade. Here is a spacious terrace with, in season, a brilliant display of summer bedding. After many years of neglect this was triumphantly instated in 1993. Experiments have been made with different colours and plants. The photographs in this book were taken in the summer of 1999 and the colour scheme is dominated by the rich blue-purple of *Heliotropium arboresecens* and the clear yellow of marigolds (*Tagetes* cultivar) planted in ribbons to follow the outlines of the beds. Silver leafed plants such as *Cerastium tomentosum* and *Senecio cineraria* (syn. *Cineraria maritima*) and spiked clumps of *Yucca gloriosa* are repeated rising on the crest of the mounded planting. At the centre of the parterres is a scal-

The aviary, of rococo trellis-work,
was completed in 1889.
The garden, with simple box-edged
beds of the rose 'Iceberg',
was designed by Lanning Roper

Waddesdon Manor

loped pool with fountains and statues of Pluto abducting Proserpine, surrounded by various mytho-logical water creatures. All these are from the same source as the north fountain. The parterre is also decorated with eighteenth century Italian white marble figures. In 1999 the gardeners experimented with a new style of carpet bedding in beds to the north and south of the pool. The idea is to com-mission distinguished living artists to make new designs each year—rather on the lines of the artists' designs for the labels of Mouton-Rothschild wine. The first design, for 2000, will be by the painter John Hubbard, with Oscar de la Renta and David Hockney making designs in the following years. Below the terrace to the south the land falls away and the grassy slopes are planted with many speci-men trees. Among the Indian horse chestnuts (*Aesculus indica*), beeches, oaks and limes are many of the newly introduced conifers which became so fashionable in the nineteenth century. Here are *Sequoia-dendron giganteum*, several cedars (*Cedrus deodara*, *Cedrus atlantica* and *Cedrus libani* subsp. *libani*) and *Thuja plicata*. Many of these have glaucous or golden foliage, which were much to the

Victorian taste, in particular intermingled with the chaste green foliage of deciduous, often native species. To many people the idea of *le goût Rothschild* bears overtones of sumptuous excess. A different way of looking at it would be to regard it as the pursuit of perfection. The contents of the house at Waddesdon —the finest furniture by the best *ébénistes* or the most beautiful Sèvres porcelain— are simply the masterpieces of the greatest craftsman in the great days of such things. If you want the best, this is the sort of thing you acquire. There is no feeling of excess in the gardens at Waddesdon, for they are very varied. There is the simplicity of the delicious rural views that open out from the top of Tree Hill. The brilliantly patterned parterre on the terrace is sumptuous, but it is exquisitely executed. The way in which beautiful pale statues are placed against rich green trees or groups of shrubs is restrained and perfectly effective. The most elaborate features of the garden, the aviary and the parterre, are placed in the wider landscape of trees and grass. In the Rothschild family the expression 'the Waddesdon standard' was used to denote a state of perfection. The quality of gardening at Waddesdon today is close to this standard and it is something that gives pleasure to visitors of all kinds.

right

A Nereid riding the waves
in a niche on the aviary

below

Another of the eighteenth century
statues representing the four
seasons in the terrace garden

bottom right

One of the eighteenth century
statues representing the four
seasons in the terrace garden

Athelhampton House

The gardens at Athelhampton are a masterpiece of Arts and Crafts design. They were created by an architect, Francis Inigo Thomas, between 1891 and 1893 when he was in his mid twenties. The house is described by Nikolaus Pevsner in *The Buildings of England* as 'the *beau idéal* of the late medieval manor house.' It was largely built in the sixteenth century, for the Martyn family, and its essential original character survives. In 1891 the estate was bought by Alfred Cart de Lafontaine who commissioned Thomas to carry out improvements to the house and to create a new garden. Little is known of any earlier garden here and certainly there seems to have been nothing of any special merit. What Thomas devised takes as its first cue, as in all successful garden designs, the character of the house and its setting in the landscape. The house is in beautiful wooded country to the east of the town of Dorchester. Although the garden has been modified, as I shall show, it retains to this day the essence of Thomas's design.

The chief part of the garden spreads out to the east and south-east of the house, in a series of walled or hedged enclosures, each with its own atmosphere. At its heart is a circular garden, the Corona, at the point where the two axes linking the other enclosures meet. The parapet of the walls in the Corona sweeps down in a series of half-rounds with slender obelisks crowning the rising points between the sweeps. Curved beds run along the walls, attractively planted in blues, purples and whites. Here are agapanthus, several campanulas, the intense blue *Ceratostigma plumbaginoides*, *Convolvulus cneorum* and, trained against the wall, *Solanum crispum* 'Glasnevin'. A circular pool at the centre has an urn and a water jet and finely decorated stone piers flank wrought-iron gates leading into the four gardens that lead off it.

The entrance forecourt
to Athelhampton House

above

The lily pond below the eastern
façade of the house

right

The Corona Garden with its fine
stonework set off by yew hedging

The Great Court is a square with a sunken lawn on which are disposed twelve giant pyramids of yew – now 30ft high. On the south-west side is a raised walk running the whole width of the garden, with at each end a stone pavilion with a steeply pitched roof and beautifully detailed pilasters. Beds of lemon-yellow flowered *Potentilla fruticosa* run along either side of the paving leading up to the pavilions. At the centre of the terrace a stone bench is set into a recess in the wall, commanding views over the garden. Along the garden side of the terrace walk a stone balustrade is ornamented with obelisks crowning the top of each pier. Below the balustrade, on either side of very broad steps, is a narrow runnel of water into which lion's masks set in the wall spout jets of water. In summer, lemon trees in terracotta pots are arranged along the edge of the runnel. There is a feeling of mystery and drama about the Great Court, emphasised by the stage-like terrace. The garden originally had a series of rather fussy zig-zag beds let into the turf and embracing each of the clipped yews. As the yews grew to their great size they began to encroach on the beds which were suppressed. The resulting simplicity is far more beautiful. Beyond the far side of the Corona, spread out below the east façade of the house, is a stately rectangular enclosure with a gently sunken lawn and a long canal, or lily pond, with rounded ends and a single leaping water jet in the middle. A painting of the garden published in *The Studio* in 1901 shows four yew pyramids marking the corners of this enclosure, of exactly the same shape as those in the Great Court. It is not known if, in fact, these were ever planted. Restraint is the atmosphere here, with the only drama coming from a magnificent cedar of Lebanon (*Cedrus libani* subsp. *libani*) spreading its limbs over the garden walls close to the house.

In the space to the east of the Corona *The Studio* painting shows a central path with parterre-like beds on either side. Today the beds have been replaced with mixed planting with such exotics as *Callistemon citrinus*, *Trachycarpus fortunei* and *Eucalyptus dalrympleana* which seem a little bold and brassy for so small a space. At the far end of this enclosure a fountain and pool in a Gothic niche are let into the wall with a broadly curving pool below, all of which were part of Thomas's design.

The enclosures I have described form the heart of Thomas's original design. Their success comes from their strength and simplicity, with every detail of architecture, masonry, ironwork, hedges and topiary exceptionally finely made. Yet it was not an easy site, for it slopes downwards, rather awkwardly, from south to north. Thomas solved this problem and made it into a virtue, with all the aplomb of a magician plucking a white rabbit out of a hat. The Corona links the levels, with steps rising steeply up to the Great Court and on the opposite side more gently down to the pool garden. Beyond Thomas's garden are recent additions which serve only to sharpen one's appreciation of his own masterly design. Here are formal elements – a pleached lime walk, a canal, an octagonal pool, a formal rose garden and so on. A pair of mixed borders flanks a path leading to a statue of Queen Victoria – but the borders are much too narrow for the substantial scale of their planting. Compared with the harmony and logic of Thomas's design – never mind the beauty of its details – these later gardens are an incoherent jumble. I have seen a visitor emerge into this part of the garden with a frown on his face, puzzled by the abrupt change in mood and uncertain where he should go next. In Thomas's time this area was simple woodland, with a path running along the outside of the garden wall with gateways allowing glimpses of the woods.

Thomas's masterly design at Athelhampton exemplifies the principle, of universal truth in laying out a garden, that if you get the bones right, nothing else matters much. The corollary, alas, is also true: if you get the bones wrong, nothing can save the garden.

Athelhampton House

above

One of the pavilions on the terrace

overlooking the Great Court

right

A view from the centre

of the terrace of the Great Court

The house is firmly related to its
surroundings by the garden

facing page

In the 'tropical' garden, laid out in
the former rose garden, strong
contrasts of foliage are associated
with dramatic veils of colour –
purple *Verbena bonariensis*, cannas
and brilliant dahlia

The house at Great Dixter dates from the very end of the fifteenth
century. In 1910 it was greatly expanded, by the addition of another timber-framed house of a slightly later period and by much work
by the architect Sir Edwin Lutyens. His client was Nathaniel Lloyd,
a printer who became fascinated by architecture and followed the
conversion of his house with special interest. In middle age he
trained as an architect, being elected Fellow of the Royal Institute
of British Architects in 1933 at the age of 64. Apart from the
charms of the house, marvellously built of brick, half-timbering
and old tiles, the outhouses and various yards had great potential as a garden. Lloyd and Lutyens in
partnership devised a framework for the layout which has proved its worth, as the subsequent planting shows. Lloyd's wife, whose maiden name was the delightfully appropriate Daisy Field, was a
most skilled and knowledgeable plantswoman. This combination of the designing husband and
plantswoman wife has produced countless good English gardens. In this case the formula was
extended, for their youngest son, Christopher, became an outstanding gardener, one of the most
influential gardener/writers of his day.

When Nathaniel Lloyd bought Dixter (as it was then called) there was little of horticultural interest, except for two orchards. Lloyd took a particular interest in hedges and topiary, which greatly
enrich the structure of the garden to this day. He became most knowledgeable about the two great
hedging and topiary plants, yew (*Taxus baccata*) and box (*Buxus sempervirens*), and wrote an excellent book on the subject, *Garden Craftsmanship in Yew and Box* (1923). The essential layout of the
garden conformed to the Arts and Crafts principle of a series of garden rooms of architectural character. There is no attempt to create the kind of carefully worked out harmony between house and

left

Fine hedges and topiary were laid
out just before World War I

below and facing page
The 'tropical' garden, full of drama
and colour, is set in the context
of ancient outhouses

garden that the Renaissance designer would have thought essential. The house, for a start, is highly irregular and the harmony that exists in the garden layout comes from the repeated use of vernacular building materials – brick and clay tiles in this part of England – and of yew and box. Having said that, there are bold axial vistas, leading up to the front door of the house and leading south-east along the Long Border behind the house. These locate the house and its outhouses very strongly in their designed setting.

Although Nathaniel and Daisy Lloyd created the framework of the garden at Great Dixter, it is their son Christopher who has given it its essential character today. He was born in 1921 and, apart from service in World War II, has spent his whole life here. He trained in horticulture at Wye College, where he later taught, and combines to a very rare degree a profound knowledge of practical horticulture with the most fastidious plantsmanship. He was lucky to inherit such a marvellous place in which to garden, and he has certainly made the best of it, but instead of treating it like some inviolable shrine he has been boldly experimental. As with most good gardeners, his taste, over a long gardening life, has evolved and his modern style of gardening today reflects a remarkably youthful, even irreverent, approach.

Visitors enter the garden by a simple gate and a paved path that leads straight to the front door. The house, although comprehensively reworked by Lutyens in the 20th century, is a perfect example of the vernacular English country house, before the Renaissance had its influence. The garden on either side of the path has a character of subdued charm – the fireworks come later. Here are preserved one or two ancient trees, such as a bay (*Laurus nobilis*) and a wild pear (*Pyrus communis*). To one side of the path is a meadow garden, a swathe of grass dappled with wild flowers in their season and not mown until late in the summer to allow as many to seed as possible. This tradition of meadow gardening at Great Dixter, today widely fashionable and appropriate to concerns for ecology and organic gardening, was started by Daisy Lloyd. She was a devotee of William Robinson whose *The Wild Garden* (1870) was a much consulted book. In many parts of the garden there are naturalistic plantings in grass, often using such English native plants as *Narcissus pseudo-narcissus*, *Dactylorhiza fuchsii*, *Orchis morio* and *Anemone nemorosa* but also using many appropriate exotics. The Long Border running south-east behind the house has been one of the most influential twentieth-century garden features. Christopher Lloyd was a pioneer of the kind of border which intermingled herbaceous and woody plants – indeed, his first book was called *The Mixed Border* (1957). The Long Border at Great Dixter is over 200ft long and 15ft deep. Such substantial shrubs as the purple-leafed

above and facing page

The 'tropical' garden comes into its
own in late summer. Not all these
exotic plants are hardy – some are
given winter protection or taken
under cover

Cotinus coggygria Rubrifolius Group, the silver willow (*Salix alba* var. *sericea*) and the golden elder (*Sambucus racemosa* 'Plumosa Aurea') are underplanted with a bewildering diversity of herbaceous plants, some of them tender annuals introduced to forestall any gaps when permanent planting begins to flag.

Christopher Lloyd's intrepid style is exemplified in the changes he recently made to a formal rose garden designed by Lutyens. He kept the existing framework of old yew hedges and the intricate pattern of beds separated by stone flags but replaced the roses with a flamboyant late-season scheme. A dazzling mixture of exotic foliage – bananas (*Musa basjoo*), New Zealand flax (*Phormium tenax*) and ginger (*Hedychium flavescens*) – provides a powerful foil for the brilliant colours of dahlias, *Verbena bonariensis*, cannas and *Ipomoea lobata*. Some of these need winter protection – but this is not a cold garden, for its proximity to the sea gives it a mild micro-climate. This exotic garden, hidden away behind its ramparts of yew, comes as an explosive surprise.

In many ways Great Dixter is the archetypal English garden. It combines the love of vernacular architecture, the absence of ostentation, and abundant planting, often of rarities, within a firm framework. But Christopher Lloyd's strongly independent character and his quirky taste add a spice to what can sometimes be a rather insipid dish. Through his garden, and his admirable writings, he has had perhaps more influence than any other living gardener in England. The most valuable lesson he imparts is – make up your own mind.

Giant foliage of a banana plant
in the 'tropical' garden contrasts
with (facing page bottom)
the delicate, filigree foliage
of *Rhus pulvinata* Autumn Lace
Group; (facing page top) The Long
Border, with its ever changing
arrangement of woody and herbaceous plants, is the best known
feature of Great Dixter

Hestercombe

Sir Edwin Lutyens's orangery
in the Edwardian garden

The lake and cascade in the landscape garden with the Doric
Temple (c.1770) in the distance

Many old British estates preserve garden features of different periods. It is much less common for whole gardens of two completely different styles, alongside each other, to survive more or less intact. At Hestercombe in the county of Somerset an enchanting landscape park of the eighteenth century and a pioneer garden of the Arts and Crafts movement, made in the early years of the twentieth century, provide a juxtaposition of rare delight. Both were very nearly lost and have been brought back from the brink of extinction by two separate campaigns of restoration. The estate at Hestercombe was owned since the fourteenth century by the Warre family from whom it passed by marriage to the Bampfyldes. It was inherited in 1750 by Coplestone Warre Bampfylde, a fascinating figure of his time – a soldier, gentleman artist and landscaper who was a friend of two other landowners with a taste for landscaping, Henry Hoare II of Stourhead (see page 78) and Sir Charles Kemeys Tynte of Halswell. This trio of passionate gardeners, living quite near each other, each made landscape parks which survive and are admirable examples of their period. Bampfylde took as his site a picturesque wooded valley running down from the north towards his house. From an existing stream he created a spectacularly dramatic waterfall, plummeting over rocks on one side of the valley. The stream passes over a more gentle cascade to feed a serene pool, the Pear Pond, from which further cascades lead water towards the house. He animated the slopes on either side with ornamental buildings which also commanded fine views within his landscape. Bampfylde, an accomplished amateur artist, has left priceless views of his garden painted in the 1770s shortly after he had completed the chief work. They show close mown grass sweeping down to the undulating banks of his lake with woodland clothing the valley. His great cascade is depicted, tumbling from rocks among the trees. The indefatigable traveller, Arthur Young, visited it in 1771 and described it as a 'rural sequestered vale'. For this was no show garden, it remained throughout Bampfylde's life as a private pleasure ground and is scarcely mentioned in the voluminous contemporary literature of the eighteenth century landscape garden. After Bampfylde's death in 1791 the estate continued in his family, reverting to the Warres who remained at Hestercombe until 1872 when it was sold to Viscount Portman. He built a new, and very ugly, house to replace the Bampfylde's elegant early eighteenth century mansion. Lord Portman gave the estate to his grandson, The Hon. E.W.B. Portman, as a wedding present and it was the grandson

who, in 1903, commissioned a new garden from Sir Edwin Lutyens. Lutyens immediately recognised the beauty of the surrounding landscape – both the remains of Bampfylde's park to the north and the unspoilt rural views of the Vale of Taunton to the south. He designed the new garden on gentle slopes to the south and east of the house, directing all views away towards the countryside. In a series of brilliantly conceived terraces, animated by pools and canals, he devised one of the most beautiful gardens of its period. The site was an awkward one, dictated by the awkwardness of the house. Immediately south of the house he made a series of geometric terraces ending in a square sunken garden, over which there are views from surrounding terrace walks. The arrangement culminates in a long pergola marking the southern limit of the garden from which there are views over the countryside. To the east of the house, forming an awkward axis brilliantly connected by a circular enclosure, he added a dashing orangery. Beyond it, linked by superbly fashioned steps, is the Dutch Garden. Its northern wall is pierced by a gate whose upper half is formed of fretwork allowing views of the 18th-century landscape garden beyond, prettily framed like a picture.

Lutyens's collaborator in all this work was Gertrude Jekyll who created the strongly decorative planting plans which are so sympathetic to the harmony of Lutyens's architectural garden. One of her strengths as a garden designer was her understanding of the decorative impact of foliage, and of its associative effects on the surrounding architecture. At Hestercombe beds surrounding stone-flagged paths are edged with bergenias whose bold, rounded leaves are allowed to flop over onto the paths. A gateway is guarded by bushes of common myrtle (*Myrtus communis*) which both emphasise the architecture and soften its lines. In the Dutch Garden, with its parterre-like arrangement embellished with Renaissance-style urns, the upright forms of *Yucca gloriosa* rise above edgings of a favourite Jekyll plant *Stachys byzantina*. Much of the walling in the garden is drystone in which Miss Jekyll introduced countless suitable plants such as *Tanacetum argenteum*, pinks (*Dianthus* cultivars), snow-in-summer (*Cerastium tomentosum*) and *Sedum spathulifolium*.

above and facing page left

The restored Doric Temple occupies
a position of prominence
on the wooded slopes at the head
of the lake

Lily pools in semi-circular niches
in the Edwardian garden –
with characteristic Lutyens detail
in the stonework

In the landscape garden an urn,
dated 1786, commemorates
Bampfylde's friends Sir Charles
Kemeys Tynte and Henry Hoare

The water spout and cascade
in the landscape garden

facing page, above

A carved stone mask and water
spout in the Edwardian garden

facing page, top

Opposite it on the other side of the
valley, the Mausoleum which dates
from the 1750s

below

The long pergola which forms
the southern boundary
of the Edwardian garden

During World War II the formal gardens at Hestercombe fell into decay and remained so until 1970 when the possibility of restoring them was mooted. Somerset County Council organised the restoration with great care, most of the work being carried out in the 1970s and 80s. It was a pioneer restoration of a garden of this period which took place at a time when the tradition of Arts and Crafts gardens was being revalued.

The eighteenth century garden, however, lay neglected, known only to a few brave cognoscenti prepared to push their way through the undergrowth. In 1993 Philip White set up a trust to restore it and proceeded to raise money and mastermind the restoration with astonishing speed. Ground has been cleared, vistas opened up and surviving buildings —including a splendid mausoleum and a Doric temple, both probably designed by Bampfylde— have been beautifully restored. As landscape gardens go it is on a small scale —chamber music rather than orchestral symphony— but of delightful character.

The two gardens at the single estate of Hestercombe make a most attractive contrast. The naturalistic landscape park and the formal garden of architectural character lead into each other and make the visitor sharply aware of the charms and character of both.

Crathes Castle

The castle at Crathes was built in the old county of Kincardineshire on the east coast of Scotland in the mid sixteenth century, in a traditional style that looks to the medieval past rather than to the future. It is of the type known in Scotland as a 'tower house', rising high and crowned with cantilevered turrets, fortified and built chiefly for defensive purposes. Crathes Castle has great charm, rich in lively architectural detail and clad in pink-brown rough-cast stucco, or harling as it is called in these parts. The family that built it was called Burnard (later Burnett), English in origin, coming from Bedfordshire where they had been long established.

A garden was made at Crathes shortly after the castle was completed in the late sixteenth century. The estate is beautifully situated, commanding a fine position on slopes running down to the River Dee. Robert Gordon of Straloch wrote in the middle years of the seventeenth century describing the garden that Thomas Burnett had made: 'he has by care and skill subdued the genius of the place, for by planting firs and other trees of many kinds he has covered the forbidding crags... laid it out with gardens and clothed it with pleasance.' A later description, in 1810, is particularly interesting for what it describes may still, in essence, be seen today. George Robertson recorded 'extensive gardens, being laid out in the old-fashioned manner of straight lines, and subdivided with broad hedges of yew and holly, trimmed with the utmost regularity, and exhibiting in some places, the fanciful resemblance of chairs, pyramids, etc. Very shortly after this account an estate map gives a plan of enclosed gardens to the east and south of the castle with a layout very similar to that of the garden as it is today. These, in earlier times, would have been chiefly given over to the cultivation of fruit and vegetables but, certainly by the nineteenth century, they had been turned into pleasure gardens.

From the richly planted walled garden the castle is seen rising up

A fountain at the centre
of the upper walled garden with
its parterre of bedding plants

In the lower walled garden
a clipped Portuguese laurel
(*Prunus lusitanica*) forms a striking
eyecatcher where the borders
meet in the centre

Beyond the formal gardens by the castle, the designed setting was greatly enriched in about 1860 by the planting of many trees, deciduous and evergreen, by Sir James Horn Burnett. When the great gardener and writer Gertrude Jekyll came to see Crathes Castle in 1895 she admired the flower gardens which she described as being 'quite modern.' She was particularly taken with the dazzling colours: 'The brilliancy of colours in these Scottish gardens is something remarkable. Whether it is attributable to soil or climate one cannot say; possibly the greater length of day, and therefore of daily sunshine, may account for it.' She did notice, however, that flowering was much later than in southern English gardens. The borders which Miss Jekyll admired are illustrated, giving precious information on their appearance at that time, in the watercolour paintings by G.S. Elgood that illustrate her book *Some English Gardens* (1904).

In the twentieth century the greatest contribution to the appearance of the garden was made by Sir James and Lady Burnett. Sir James was a friend of the great nurseryman and plant connoisseur Harold Hillier, under whose influence he greatly enriched the range of shrubs and trees grown. After 1926, Sybil Burnett, perhaps influenced by the writings of Gertrude Jekyll, began to lay out flower borders with carefully deployed colour schemes which are preserved today. The Burnetts' ownership of the estate ended in 1951 when they passed it over to the National Trust for Scotland.

The whole of the pleasure gardens are enclosed in walls, but within it there is a difference of levels, providing raised views of the lower garden. A magnificent double yew walk running southwards from the castle divides the area. Tradition gives these yew hedges the date of 1702, but there is no documentary evidence for this exact dating. The plants are certain to be old, so the traditional dating is not certainly wrong, and they could well be the hedges referred to by George Robertson in 1810. He refers to topiary and, indeed, the yew hedges today have giant, curiously organic topiary shapes bursting out from their crests.

One of Lady Burnett's most successful new arrangements was the Upper Pool, or Colour, garden. Immediately below the southern façade of the castle a square pool is framed in four right-angled yew hedges. The surrounding beds follow this four-part layout but have a brilliant colour scheme, making a splendid foil to the crisp structural geometry of pool and hedges. Scarlet nasturtiums (*Tropaeolum majus* cultivars) and potentillas intermingle with swathes of yellow achilleas and daylilies (*Hemerocallis* cultivars) and orange ligularias and heleniums. At the centre the surface of the pool sparkles alongside the sombre green of the yews.

In the lower garden Lady Burnett carried out other experimental colour harmony plantings. The whole area has a quadripartite layout, quite possibly following the traditional pattern of vegetable gardens with cruciform paths. At the centre of the four divisions is an old Portugal (*Prunus lusitanica*) which has been clipped into a bold domed shape. On two sides the paths are lined with herbaceous beds restricted to white flowers. These ghostly and memorable borders were created as early as 1936, long predating Vita Sackville-West's celebrated White Garden at Sissinghurst Castle which was not made until after World War II. One pair of herbaceous borders in the lower gardens survives from the nineteenth century. Blues and mauves of phlox and campanulas are spiked with brilliant dabs of scarlet and richer purple illuminated with the occasional yellow, like a shaft of sunlight. Scottish gardens seem to handle colour in a distinctively lively way. Indeed, tartan, the national textile, is a celebration of the native genius for colour.

Walking among the lavish borders of the lower garden in high summer the visitor may see one of the most memorable garden settings in Britain. The giant yew hedges are visible above the borders, crowned with their curious topiary decorations, and high above them is the castle itself, rearing up and playing its own spectacular part in the whole ornamental scheme.

facing page

Ancient yew hedges, with their
curiously shaped topiaries, divide
the walled garden and make
a handsome background to
the borders

In the lower walled garden are
colour themed borders of brilliant
reds and purples

left from top to bottom

Colour themed gardens in the
walled garden - blue and lavender,
and white; blue also dominates
the seasonal planting in
the upper garden parterre

In the Upper Pool Garden strong
blocks of clipped yew dominate
the layout with its brilliant colour
scheme of scarlet, yellow
and orange

Beth Chatto's Garden

Beth Chatto is a nurserywoman and garden writer who has had a great influence on garden design in England towards the end of the twentieth century. She first caught the imagination of gardeners by her brilliant displays at plant shows, in particular those organised by the Royal Horticultural Society in London. Her displays broke entirely with tradition for, instead of arranging the plants in neatly regimented rows, she created marvellous naturalistic arrangements of breathtaking beauty. Furthermore, she emphasised the habitats of the plants – always grouping them according to their natural environments. Thus, for example, plants for hot dry sites, or moist shady sites, would be grouped together thus revealing the common characteristics of plants from similar habitats. Although she showed great artistry in her arrangements, an additional, perhaps unexpected, harmony came from the fact that the plants came from similar habitats. Regardless of the part of the world from which a plant comes, the appearance of many plants will be a reflection of their habitats. For example, many plants from dry, windy places are covered in very fine hairs which prevent excessive loss of moisture. These fine hairs are the source of the pale grey foliage which we admire in many plants from the Mediterranean region (for example species of lavender or of *Santolina*). But plants from similarly dry habitats in Australasia or the Near East have evolved precisely the same characteristic for the same reason.

In the water garden the banks of pools are densely planted with moisture-loving plants

Hostas line a path in the water
garden with white foxgloves
forming punctuation marks

right

right
A silver birch (*Betula pendula*)
ornaments a sweeping lawn in the
water garden

This concern for the habitat of plants is an essential part of the skilful gardener's approach to his craft and it is also very much in accord with our new concern for the future of the environment. Plants in the wrong site will never look right and plants from different habitats, carelessly intermingled, will strike a disharmonious note. These are things that many gardeners understand intuitively but Beth Chatto's great contribution to gardening has been to spell out the underlying principles in a most systematic way. Her two earliest books, *The Dry Garden* and *The Damp Garden*, described plants suitable for those habitats. The catalogue of her nursery, which she started in 1967, lists plants scrupulously according to their preferred sites. Lastly, and perhaps most influentially, she has put her theories into practice in her own garden which adjoins the nursery. Here, a visitor may see the plants which he or she likes, most skilfully deployed in the garden. Beth Chatto's garden is near Colchester in Essex on the east coast of England, a part of the country which enjoys the lowest rainfall in Britain, rarely exceeding 20 inches per annum and often very much less than that. Part of the garden is laid out in a gentle depression which, when Beth Chatto came here over 30 years ago, had a spring-fed ditch into which water from the surrounding fields would also drain. Here she has been able to construct a series of naturalistic pools by damming the ditch, and to plant many trees of an appropriate kind, in order to create the damp shade which is favourable to so many desirable garden plants. There were already some good trees here taking advantage of the moist site — in particular willows (*Salix* species) and alders (*Alnus* species). Some ancient oaks (*Quercus robur*) provided magnificent ornaments to the upper levels of the garden. Within this framework a thrilling landscape has been developed in which the plants flourish in their carefully chosen sites.

The margins of the pools are lavishly clothed in plants. Many of these have dramatic foliage, such as *Rheum palmatum* 'Atropurpureum', *Gunnera tinctoria*, *Lysichiton americanus* and many ferns and hostas. These are enlivened by appropriate flowering plants — Candelabra primulas (such as *P. bulleyana* and *P. japonica*), irises (such as *I. sibirica* and *I. laeivigata*) and astilbes. The style of planting is naturalistic but these plants, coming from so many different parts of the world, would have never been seen together in nature. It is their need for the same growing conditions that makes them such harmonious partners.

148

An extreme contrast to the water garden is the gravel garden which was started in 1991. This 3/4 acre space was formerly the nursery car-park, at a higher level than the water garden, with very poor soil of sandy gravel. In the 1980s there was a sequence of very dry summers in England, and growing anxieties about a radical change in the climate caused by global warming. These hot, rainless summers caused particular problems for gardeners in the driest parts of the country. Irrigation is both expensive and offends the conservationist feelings of many gardeners. Beth Chatto decided, as an experiment, to create a garden which would flourish with no artificial irrigation. She ploughed the compacted surface of the carpark and added compost to enable young plants to establish themselves in the largely humus-free soil. Plants were chosen for their ability to survive long periods with no rain, and evaporation from the soil was slowed down by laying down a thick mulch of gravel. The gravel makes an excellent medium for seeds to germinate – because of the moisture immediately below the upper layer. Beth Chatto wanted to create a naturalistic layout, with plants forming self-sustaining communities, scattering themselves as they do in nature in places that favour them. Many shrubs are used, especially those from Mediterranean countries like *Phlomis*, *Santolina*, *Lavandula*, *Cistus* and *Atriplex halimus*. Such herbaceous perennials as species of *Euphorbia*, *Diascia*, *Artemisia*, *Anthemis*, *Linaria* and others form a spreading layer about the feet of shrubs. Countless bulbs were introduced, especially of those sorts that self-sow such as *Crocus*, several species of *Allium*, tulips, *Scilla* and *Chionodoxa*. In high summer it presents a sight of astonishing floriferous vigour but in any season it has its beauty. In the heart of winter the dead top growth, and ornamental seed pods have an austere charm of their own. The experiment has been a resounding success, both creating a landscape of unusual beauty and proving the virtues, much in agreement with the taste of our time, of gardening in collaboration with nature.

In the gravel garden ornamental grasses, grey foliage plants and seedheads make a universally decorative background to the profusion of often self-sown plants which are 'edited' where necessary

left

A tall plant of *Euphorbia characias*
subsp. *wulfenii* rises among
catmint, pink cistus and the silver
foliage of *Artemisia* 'Powis Castle'

below

In the woodland garden the crisp
foliage of *Iris sibirica* stands out
among swathes of Himalayan
primulas, hostas and ferns

below

Dense planting of Himalayan
primulas and the bold foliage
of *Hosta sieboldiana elegans*
in the woodland garden

right

In the gravel garden red
Penstemon 'Andenken an Friedrich
Hahn', white lilies and contrasting
planting of tall grass and rounded
foliage of bergenia

The giant seed heads of *Allium christophii* and red penstemon in the gravel garden

Beth Chatto's Garden

Opening Details

Note: All the gardens described in this book are open regularly to the public. These are the usual opening times, but they may fluctuate from year to year. Consult an up-to-date guide such as Patrick Taylor's *Sunday Telegraph Guide to the Gardens of Britain & Ireland* (Dorling Kindersley) or telephone the number given.

Athelhampton House, Athelhampton, Dorchester DT2 7LG, Dorset, England

Tel: 01305 848363
Fax: 01305 848135
Open from March to end October, daily except Saturday 10.30-5;
from November to end February, Sunday 10.30-5

Bowood, Calne SN11 0LZ, Wiltshire, England

Tel: 01249 812102
Open from April to end of October, daily 10-6

Bramham Park, Wetherby LS23 6ND, West Yorkshire, England

Tel: 01937 844265
Fax: 01937 845923
Open from end of June to beginning of September on Sunday, Tuesday,
Wednesday and Thursday 1.15-5.30

Caerhays Castle, near Gorran FA1 7DE, Cornwall, England

Tel: 01872 501310
Fax: 01872 501870
Open from mid March to mid May, Monday to Friday 11-4

Beth Chatto Gardens, Elmstead Market, Colchester CO7 7DB, Essex, England

Tel: 01206 822007
Fax: 01206 825933
Open from beginning March to end of October, daily except Sunday 9-5;
from beginning November to end of February, daily except Saturday
and Sunday 9-4

Crathes Castle, near Banchory AB31 3QJ, Grampian, Scotland

Tel: 01330 844525
Fax: 01330 844797
Open daily 9-sunset

Great Dixter, Northiam, Rye TN31 6PH, East Sussex, England

Tel: 01797 252878
Fax: 01797 252879
Open from April to mid October, daily except Monday 2-5

Hampton Court, East Molesey KT8 9AU, Surrey, England

Tel: 0181 781 9500
Fax: 0181 781 9509
Open daily from dawn to dusk (Privy Garden open 9.30-6, closes 4.30 in winter)

Hatfield House, Hatfield AL9 5NQ, Hertfordshire, England

Tel: 01707 262823
Fax: 01707 275719
Open from end of March to end of September, daily except Monday 11-6

Hestercombe, Cheddon Fitzpaine, near Taunton TA2 8LQ, Somerset, England

Tel: 01823 413923
Open daily 10-6

Kinross House, Kinross KY13 7ET, Tayside, Scotland

Open from May to end of September 10-7

Levens Hall, Kendall LA8 0PD, England

Tel: 01539 560321
Fax: 01539 560669
Open from April to mid October, daily except Friday and Saturday 10-5

Montacute House, Montacute TA15 6XP, Somerset, England

Tel: 01935 823289
Open from end of March to end of September daily except Tuesday 11-5.30
(closed on Monday and Tuesday in winter; opening hours 11.30-4)

Penshurst Place, Penshurst, near Tonbridge TN11 8DG, Kent, England

Tel: 01892 870307
Fax: 01892 870866
Open from end of March to end of October, daily 11-6

Powis Castle, Welshpool SY21 8RF, Powys, Wales

Tel: 01938 554336
Open from the end of March to the end of October, daily except Monday and
Tuesday 11-6 (July and August, also open Tuesday)

Stourhead, Stourton, Warminster BA12 6QH, Wiltshire, England

Tel: 01747 840348
Open: daily 9-7 or sunset if earlier (usually closed for a few days at end of July)

Stowe, Buckingham MK18 5EH, Buckinghamshire, England

Tel: 01280 822850
Open from end March to mid April daily 10-5; from mid April to early July,
Monday, Wednesday, Friday and Sunday, 10-5; early July to beginning
September, daily 10-5; early September to end October, Monday, Wednesday,
Friday and Sunday 10-5

Studley Royal, Fountains, Ripon HG4 3DZ, North Yorkshire, England

Tel: 01765 608888
Open daily 10-7 (in winter closes at 5 and sometimes closed on Friday)

Tresco Abbey, Tresco, Isles of Scilly TR24 0QQ, Cornwall, England

Tel: 01720 422849
Fax: 01720 422868
Open daily 10-4

Waddesdon Manor, Waddesdon, near Aylesbury HP18 0JH, Buckinghamshire, England

Tel: 01296 651211
Fax: 01296 651293
Open from early March to end December, Wednesday to Sunday 10-5

Bibliography

General

Mavis Batey and David Lambert, *The English Garden Tour: a View into the Past* (1990)

Ray Desmond, *Bibliography of British Gardens* (1988)

Miles Hadfield, Robert Harling and Leonie Higton (eds), *British Gardeners: a Biographical Dictionary* (1980)

Miles Hadfield, *Gardening in Britain* (1960)

Penelope Hobhouse, *Plants in Garden History* (1992)

John Dixon Hunt and Peter Willis (eds), *The Genius of the Place: the English Landscape Garden 1620-1820* (1975)

Geoffrey Jellicoe, Susan Jellicoe, Patrick Goode and Michael Alexander(eds.), *The Oxford Companion to Gardens* (1986)

Christopher Thacker, *The Genius of Gardening: the History of Gardens in Britain and Ireland* (1994)

The Middle Ages

John Harvey, *Mediaeval Gardens* (1981)

Teresa McLean, *Medieval English Gardens* (1989)

The Renaissance

Roy Strong, *The Renaissance Garden in England* (1979)

The Eighteenth Century

David Jacques, *Georgian Gardens: The Reign of Nature* (1983)

Mark Laird, *The Flowering of the English Landscape Garden* (1999)

Dorothy Stroud, *Capability Brown* (1975)

The Nineteenth Century

Brent Elliott, *Victorian Gardens* (1986)

The Twentieth Century

Jane Brown, *Gardens of a Golden Afternoon: The Story of a Partnership: Edwin Lutyens and Gertrude Jekyll* (1982)

David Ottewill, *The Edwardian Garden* (1989)

Russell Page, *The Education of a Gardener* (1962)

Biographical Notes

Beaumont, Guillaume

Born c. 1650, died 1727. French garden designer about whom little
is known. Worked for King James II at Hampton Court and for Colonel
James Grahme at Bagshot and Levens Hall.

Bridgeman, Charles

Born c. 1670, died c.1738. Designer of grand formal gardens, becoming
less formal later in his career. Worked at Chiswick House, Claremont,
Cliveden, Hampton Court, Rousham, Wimpole Hall and elsewhere.

Brown, Lancelot 'Capability'

Born 1716, died 1783. The most important English 18th-century landscape designer who created naturalistic landscapes on the grand scale
and spawned many imitators. He designed parks at, among many other
places, Alnwick Castle, Audley End, Blenheim Palace, Bowood, Chatsworth,
Croome Court, Harewood House, Longleat, Petworth and Stowe.

Bruce, Sir William

Born 1630, died 1710. Scottish architect and garden designer. Worked
on the royal palace at Holyroodhouse, at Hopetoun House and at
his own estates of Balcaskie and Kinross.

Caus, Salomon de

Born c.1576, died 1626. French Huguenot garden designer, engineer
(especially hydraulic) and author. Worked in England at Greenwich
Palace, Hatfield House, Richmond Palace and Somerset House.

Chatto, Beth

Born 1923. Very influential nurserywoman, plantswoman and author.
The proprietor of a nursery specialising in herbaceous perennials
and the creator of an influential garden.

Emes, William

Born 1730, died 1803. Landscape designer in the tradition of Capability
Brown. Worked at Belton House, Bowood, Hawkstone Park, Powis Castle,
Tatton Park, Wimpole Hall and many other estates, especially those
on the English/Welsh border.

Jekyll, Gertrude

Born 1843, died 1932. Garden designer, artist and author. Deeply knowledgeable gardener and plantswoman who had profound effect on the
design of borders. Often worked in partnership with Sir Edwin Lutyens.
Worked at The Deanery, Folly Farm, Lindisfarne Castle, Marsh Court,
Munstead Wood, Vann.

Kent, William

Born 1685, died 1748. Architect, artist and garden designer. Key figure
in the transition between formality and the informal landscape park.
Worked at Badminton, Chiswick House, Houghton Hall, Rousham
(his masterpiece) and Stowe.

Lloyd, Christopher

Born 1921. The most influential English garden writer of the post-war
period. Owner of the garden at Great Dixter, distinguished plantsman
and powerful eminence grise.

Lutyens, Sir Edwin

Born 1869, died 1944. Architect and, especially in partnership with
Gertrude Jekyll, designer of gardens of architectural character placing
much emphasis on the vernacular tradition. Worked at Castle Drogo,
Folly Farm, Great Dixter, Hestercombe, Little Thakeham, Orchards and
many other estates.

Marot, Daniel

Born 1661, died 1752. French, Huguenot, architect and garden designer
especially associated with King William III in both the Netherlands
(Het Loo and several other aristocratic estates) and England (Hampton
Court Palace, especially the Privy Garden, before 1702).

Reiss, Mrs F.E. (Phyllis)

Born c.1888, died 1961. Knowledgeable plantswoman and amateur
garden designer. Owner with her husband of Tintinhull House, Somerset,
1933-61. Made an influential garden of compartments at Tintinhull
and advised on the borders at Montacute House, Somerset.

Repton, Humphry

Born 1752, died 1818. The most important landscape designer after
the period of 'Capability' Brown, evolving a distinctive picturesque style.
Worked at Antony, Blaise Castle, Bowood, Bulstrode, Endsleigh,
Sheringham Park, Tatton Park and many other estates.

Roper, Lanning

Born 1912, died 1983. American garden designer, especially of borders,
who practised in Britain. Worked at Broughton Castle, Claverton Manor,
Glenveagh Castle, Penshurst Place, Waddesdon Manor and many other
gardens in Britain and Ireland.

Sackville-West, Victoria (Vita)

Born 1892, died 1962. Influential gardener and writer who, with
her husband Harold Nicolson, created the garden at Sissinghurst Castle.

Thomas, Graham Stuart

Born 1909. Nurseryman, author, garden designer and Gardens Adviser
to the National Trust between 1955 and 1974. A figure of commanding
importance in British horticulture in the post-war period.

Tradescant, John (the elder)

Born c.1570, died 1638. Gardener to Robert Cecil, first earl of Salisbury,
at Hatfield House, 1610-15; gardener to Edward, Lord Wotton,
St Augustine's, Canterbury, 1615; travelled with Sir Dudley Digges
to Russia, 1618; travelled in Mediterranean, 1620; gardener to Duke
of Buckingham at New Hall, 1622-c.1629; Keeper of the Gardens to King
Charles I, 1630-8.

Tradescant, John (the younger)

Born 1608, died 1662. Succeeded father as gardener to King Charles I,
1638, Travelled to Virginia (1637, 1642, 1654) and introduced many
North American plants to Europe.

Vanbrugh, Sir John

Born 1664, died 1726. Architect, garden designer and playwright.
Designer of many Baroque gardens for houses that he had designed
at Blenheim Palace, Castle Howard, Eastbury, Grimsthorpe Castle,
Kingsweston, Seaton Delaval and Stowe.

Printed by STIGE S.p.A.

Torino – Italy – September 2001